ENJOY YOUR BIBLE

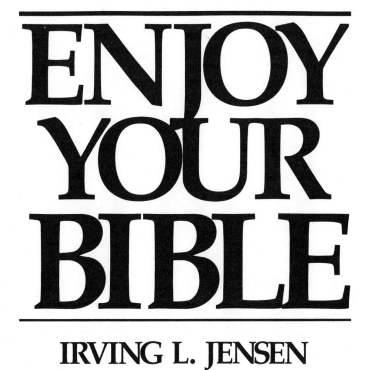

ENJOY YOUR BIBLE

IRVING L. JENSEN

World Wide Publications
A ministry of the Billy Graham Evangelistic Association
1303 Hennepin Ave., Minneapolis, MN 55403

Enjoy Your Bible

© 1969 by Irving L. Jensen

Originally published in 1969 by The Moody Bible Institute of Chicago.

World Wide Publications is the publishing ministry of the Billy Graham Evangelistic Association.

ISBN: 0-89066-146-4

Printed in the United States of America

Contents

"Were not our hearts *burning within us* while he talked with us on the road and *opened the Scriptures* to us?"

(Luke 24:32, emphasis added)

Introduction

Reading and studying the Bible is a basic requirement for your growth as a Christian; and, happily, it can be one of the most enjoyable experiences of your day.

Why don't we fully enjoy the Bible? Perhaps it's because we haven't felt the delight of first–hand discoveries of the Bible's priceless gems. We absorb much of what is spoken or written by others, but aren't moved to search on our own.

Confucius, the Chinese teacher of ancient days, said, "I give a pupil one corner of a subject, and if he cannot find the other three corners, I do not want him to be my pupil." Apply this to Bible study and the question arises, *What will motivate students to study on their own?*

Whatever this motivation is, it is clear that it must involve all three of the God–given aspects of personality: intellect, emotion, and will. Bible study can be truly enjoyable when it challenges your intellect, stirs your emotions, and directs your will. As professor of a biblical studies course, I once overheard a student remark, "This makes Bible study fun!" He'd begun to experience the excitement of discovering truths in the Bible he'd never seen before. Things were stirring up inside of him, captivating his intellect and will. He was enjoying the Bible!

We're all created with something inside us that's attracted to enjoyment and satisfaction. The world finds its expression in the pleasures of sin, temporary though they be. *Can* a good and pure activity, like Bible study be *truly* pleasurable? The answer is yes. Since the Bible was written, believers have testified to such satisfaction. The psalmist called his pulse–quickening experience with

God's Word a "delight" (Psalm 119:24). The same Lord who inflamed the hearts of two disciples as he "opened the Scriptures to them" on the road to Emmaus (Luke 24:32) offers this exhilarating invitation to you today.

Think of your Bible study as a hunt for buried treasure. The pages ahead include charts and proven methods to guide you on your way. Should you become discouraged by rough terrain ahead, feel free to lighten your load by charting an unscheduled side–trip. The important thing to remember is, the Bible is inspired by God—the same God that dwells in you through his Holy Spirit. Jesus promised to give us his Holy Spirit, to be with us always (John 14:16). The Bible is actually living communication from the Holy Spirit. Because of this, Bible study can be instructive, comforting, challenging and inspiring—and it's open to all. "For everyone who asks receives; he who seeks finds; and to him who knocks, the door will be opened" (Matthew 7:8). Begin now to really enjoy your Bible!

PART I
Getting to Know the Bible

1
Appreciating the Bible

Today, we know that countless millions own at least one copy of the Scriptures, but no one knows what proportion of these fully appreciate their treasure. Yet, appreciation of the Bible is a first step to enjoying it.

What is the Bible, anyway? Where did it come from? Who wrote it? How did it get here? What does it say? What makes it such a unique book? To find some answers, we'll begin at its source.

I. A Miraculous Book

We all know that the Bible is a book of miracles, in that it records miracles. But are we aware that the very existence of the Bible is a miracle in itself? Let's take a closer look at this matchless phenomenon.

A. Its Author

W. E. Gladstone said, "The Bible is stamped with a specialty of origin, and an immeasurable distance separates it from all competitors." Just as no one can fully understand the miracle of human birth, so no one can fully understand the miraculous birth of God's book, the Bible. God says the Bible came into being by his *breath* (2 Timothy 3:16), which is also how his universe was created (Psalm 33:6).

God further says that the human authors of the Scriptures "spoke from God as they were carried along by the Holy Spirit" (2 Peter 1:21). Although they had the free exercise of their native abilities, emotions, thoughts, and vocabularies, what they wrote is worthy of our trust, because "they were carried along by the Holy Spirit." The human writers themselves were fallible, but their work in composing the Bible was infallible, because of this divine control.

B. Its transmission

The Scriptures were handed down to each succeeding generation first by the spoken and later by the written word. The ancient scribes making copies of the books of the Bible occasionally committed errors of eye, ear, or memory; for their work, unlike that of the original authors, was not infallible. But this type of minor copy error never impinged on the overall integrity of the corpus of manuscripts. The purity of the Bible text is higher than that suggested by the famous soap slogan, "ninety–nine and forty–four one–hundredths percent pure." No other writing, exposed to similar time and modes of transmission, has survived so intact. Only God's master control over the scribal processes can account for this.

C. Its growth into one single book

The Bible includes sixty–six books, written by about forty authors over a period of some fifteen hundred years. In ways known only to God, and under his superintendence, these books are now bound together in one volume. And they are more than just a collection of diverse writings. Despite the vast span of time and human personality that went into its composition, the Bible has one major theme: the salvation of God offered to sinful man by Jesus Christ.

D. Its survival

Apathy and disuse, worm and rot (even the command of a Roman emperor, Diocletian, in A.D. 303, that all the Scriptures be destroyed by fire), have not succeeded in removing the Bible from the scene. In the words of the prophet, "The grass withers, the flower fades, but the word of our God stands forever" (Isaiah 40:8). Today millions revere the Bible as God's inspired word despite the subtle attempts by liberal theologians to interpret it narrowly as a mere product of man. It has survived the hammer blows of the skeptics of the ages. The inscription on the monument to the Huguenots of Paris expresses this so vividly: "Hammer away, ye hostile hands; your hammers break; God's anvil stands."

E. Its influence

The Bible is the most published book in the world because the world continues to seek its counsel and revelation of the truth. Six million copies of *Good News for Modern Man* (*Today's English Version*) were in circulation within a year of its publication, despite the fact that there had been no special promotion in advance of its appearance.

Of all the books ever written, the Bible is the only one that fully understands man. Its phenomenal impact on the souls of men, the hearths of homes, and the halls of nations can be recognized, but never fully measured. This is because it is more than a book—it is the very life–giving breath of God.

Truly the Bible *is* a miracle book! And from a practical standpoint the most wonderful thing about this is that *God gave this miracle book to us for our own personal benefit*, to show us where we came from, where we're going, and how to live in the meantime.

II. A Manual for Living

Have you ever thought of the Bible as being a manual that goes along with the "product," which is *you*? The book and you are meant to go together—to be inseparable. Both were brought into being by the same breath of God (Genesis 2:7; 2 Timothy 3:16). The Bible was given *for* you, to go *with* you. This is clearly God's design.

When God put man and woman on earth, he didn't leave them here without instructions. In the Garden of Eden, it was by *audible* conversation that he communicated guidance to them. Then, for all centuries, there would be primarily *Spirit to spirit* communion. But *written* language became another way that God chose to in-

struct men and women on how to live. And so, over a period of one–and–a–half millenia, God caused a book to be
written, by human beings—inspired by the Holy Spirit—a
book intended to "go with" man.

A. Our Maker

Most of the Bible was written to tell about our Creator
and Savior . . . who he is, what kind of heart he has, what
he does. Human words cannot fully describe him, for he
is infinite and eternal in all his attributes. But in picture
words (even "Spirit"—*wind*—and "Christ"—*anointed*—
are picture words), and in men's testimonies of their deal-
ings with him, we are given all we need to know of our
Maker. He is Wonderful Counselor, Mighty God, Ever-
lasting Father, Prince of Peace. He does all things well.
Nothing is too hard for him. In him all things are held together. He loves man with an infinite love.

B. Our present life

The Bible is our instruction book on how to live in this
life, with a view to the life beyond. It is a book of deep and
infinite truths. But it speaks its vital message of salvation
and Christian living in such a way that even a child can
respond.

The Bible warns against negligence of things present
and apathy toward things to come. It says you *must* be
born again if you are to find real joy and lasting peace.
According to the Bible, estrangement from God spells
lack of fulfillment in this life. True satisfaction is found
through the filling and indwelling of the Holy Spirit: "The
Spirit has given us life; he must also control our lives"
(Galatians 5:25, TEV).

The Bible offers moral instruction: "How can a young
man keep his way pure? By living according to your word"
(Psalm 119:9). We are not to abuse body, soul, or spirit,
but present these to God. To the person who follows
God's moral instruction in the Bible, he promises abundant joys and rivers of living water.

Sadly, some of us carry the mistaken impression that
the Bible is a dry, irrelevant collection of impractical information—beautiful on a coffee table, but certainly not

"must" reading for our busy lives. When things go wrong in life, we're often prone to by–pass God and go everywhere else for help. We go to psychiatrists, psychologists, advisers, and friends. We take tranquilizers and try talk–yourself–out–of–it therapies. We consult God only as a last resort—but, if we were really wise, we would *run* to him at the first sign of trouble.

God is the source of all help for his creation. He is truly the Master Mechanic for the human being! He knows the machine he has made, and he has a warehouse of replacement parts. Bent, broken, dirty, squeaky, weak, or run–down parts are no problem to him. When King David honestly and humbly faced and confessed his sin, he was restored to his original joy and usefulness in God's service: "Restore to me the joy of your salvation and grant me a willing spirit, to sustain me. Then I will teach transgressors your ways, and sinners will turn back to you" (Psalms 51:12–13).

C. Our destiny

In one sense the Bible may be likened to a map, charting a course to heaven. It shows us that the way to heaven is through a person—Jesus Christ. It also warns of another way, a way of separation from God for rejecting his Son Jesus. That is the road to hell.

III. Manna for Strength

God wouldn't give us rules for living unless he also gave us sufficient strength to follow those directions. That strength or energy comes from the spiritual food of his Word. When God directed his people through the wilderness of Sinai, he fed them daily with manna, so that they would have the physical strength to advance. The Bible likens meditation and study of its pages to food intake for the body.

Everyone must eat, to live and grow. Any Israelite on the wilderness journey who refused to eat the manna supplied by God, perished, for there was no other food. Man will eventually die without nourishment. The Bible is our spiritual food for life and growth. Like Job we should treasure the words of God's mouth more than our physical food (Job 23:12).

We won't be hungry for God's Word if we don't acknowledge our need for that Word. An honest look into our heart should make us cry out with the psalmist, "My soul is consumed with longing for your laws at all times" (Psalm 119:20). That is "soul hunger," and it is the best kind of hunger to have.

Reading and studying the Bible should be a pleasure for all Christians. Just as the manna was sweet to the taste of the Israelites, so is the Bible to those who absorb it wholeheartedly. The psalmist experienced this: "How sweet are your words to my taste, sweeter than honey to my mouth!" (Psalm 119:103). Jeremiah said, "When your words came, I ate them; they were my joy and my heart's delight" (Jeremiah 15:16). Ezekiel discovered that even the bitter words of God, involving mourning and woe, are transformed to sweetness when taken into the soul (Ezekiel 2:8–3:3).

The Bible is "angels' food," come down from heaven, spread out on our table in the wilderness (Psalm 78:19–25). Manna in the wilderness was a daily gift of God to all his people. The supply was always there for everyone, as long as the people used what God offered. The Bible is God's ever–present gift to us. If we study it today, it will be more attractive to us tomorrow, and still more attractive the next day. God's gifts always increase in the measure of their use.

> Break Thou the bread of life, dear Lord, to me,
> As Thou didst break the loaves beside the sea;
> Beyond the sacred page I seek Thee, Lord;
> My spirit pants for Thee, O living Word.
>
> —Mary A. Lathbury

2
How to Approach the Bible

The Bible is Everyman's book. It is open to the un-
schooled and to the doctor of philosophy. Whenever a
translation of the Bible is made, the translators, adhering
faithfully to the original meaning, seek to make it livelier
to the contemporary reader. William Tyndale, who translated the first printed English New Testament (1525), had
the laity, like the "boy that driveth the plough," in mind in
all his translation work. He wrote:

> I had perceaved by experyence, how that it was impossible to
> stablysh the laye people in any truth, excepte the scripture
> were playnly layde before their eyes in their mother tonge, that
> they might se the processe, ordre and meaninge of the texte....

Bible study is for all, and the procedures of study apply equally to all. For those who are called to special min-
istries of the Word, there are refinements and extensions
of the procedures, but the basic approach in Bible study
is common to all Christians.

There lies a copy of the Bible on our desk, a veritable
invitation to blessing. It waits to be read and studied. But
how should we approach it? Here are some important
considerations to keep in mind.

I. View the Bible as a Whole Unit

The Bible is a book to be read wholly, not in part; purposefully, not haphazardly; intelligently, not unthink-
ingly. There is one overall theme: God's salvation to sinful

man through his Son, Jesus Christ. Any one part of the Bible should be read with ultimate reference to this over-all theme. Otherwise the main point of the writing will be lost.

A. Books within the Book

Keeping this unity in mind, however, we also see that the Bible is actually a library of sixty–six volumes which grew together in the course of the centuries by the guiding hand of God. Each of the human authors had a main purpose, along with subordinate motives, for composing their manuscripts. We should remember this as we read so that we don't draw conclusions without taking all of the author's intent into consideration.

These sixty–six books are works of literature, comprised of prose writings (as in the many historical books), and poetical works, (like the Psalms). When we read the narrative prose, we can expect to see plain language recounting history. Figurative language is what we can expect to encounter in the Psalms. The Epistles of the New Testament have their own unique characteristics. We may read them as personal letters revealing the great truths of God, sprinkled with practical advice for successful Christian living.

The format of a book of the Bible is like that of any other book. There are chapters, which are broken down into paragraphs; then sentences (usually the length of a verse); then words. All Bibles now follow a standard system of chapter divisions (originated by Stephen Langton in 1228) and verse divisions (originated by Robert Stephanus in 1560). Although paragraph divisions have never been standardized, the paragraph is still a convenient unit for Bible study. Most modern versions show paragraph divisions by means of some formatting device, such as indentation or asterisk.

B. A purposeful arrangement

Earlier, we referred to the Bible as a library of sixty–six volumes. When we view the Bible as a whole, we can visualize its sixty–six parts as chapters. Our question here is, are these sixty–six "chapters" arranged in our Bible in a

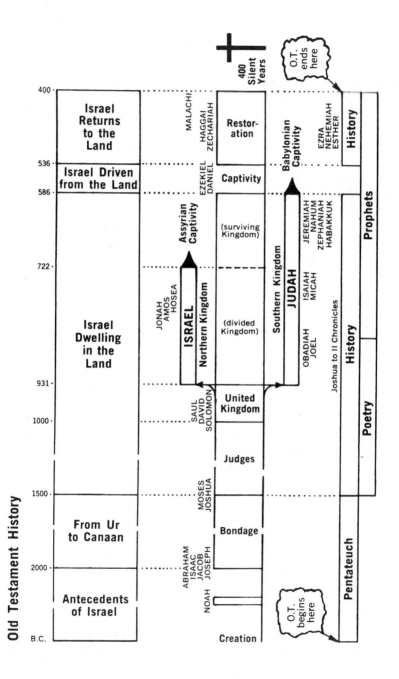

Old Testament History

purposeful pattern? The answer is yes. Each writing is located in a particular group, according to topic and type of writing. Though there is a general chronological order (from the original creation, Genesis, to the new creation, Revelation), it isn't pivotal in the overall arrangement. It is helpful, however, to know the chronological sequence of Bible history in order to appreciate the setting of each book.

1. ***The Old Testament.*** This chronological ordering applies especially to the Old Testament. The chart on page 21 shows the major eras and points of Old Testament history. Master this chart and you will find it easier to remember the setting of each Old Testament book, especially the prophetical books.

Notice where the Old Testament record begins and ends. The "four hundred silent years" refers to the lack of biblical record we have for this time. Historically, the Old Testament has four major groupings: the Pentateuch (meaning "five–fold vessel"—referring to the five "law books" of Moses), history, poetry, and prophecy. Note with what period of history (see the survey chart on page 21) these four groups are identified. The prophetical books are further broken into the Major Prophets (the five longer books of Isaiah to Lamentations) and the Minor Prophets (the twelve shorter books).

An easy way to remember the Old Testament groups is to recall the number of books in each group. The chart below shows this symmetrical arrangement:

5	12	5	5	12
PENTATEUCH	HISTORY	POETRY	MAJOR PROPHETS	MINOR PROPHETS
Genesis to Deuteronomy	Joshua to Esther	Job to Songs	Isaiah to Lamentations	Hosea to Malachi
Mainly Narrative		Mainly Reflection	Mainly Prophecy	

You will note that there are essentially only three kinds of content (narrative, reflection, prophecy), just as there are three kinds of New Testament writings (narrative, interpretation, prophecy).

It is the prophetical books of the Old Testament that are the most difficult to associate with their historical settings, because the terms Major Prophets and Minor Prophets give no clues. However, to thoroughly understand the prophetical writings, it's important to know to which of the historical groups each belongs:

a) *pre–exilic prophets:*

- prophesying to the northern kingdom (Israel): Jonah, Amos, Hosea

- prophesying to the southern kingdom (Judah): Obadiah, Joel, Isaiah, Micah, Jeremiah, Nahum, Zephaniah, Habakkuk

b) *exilic prophets:*

- Ezekiel, Daniel

c) *post–exilic prophets:*

- Haggai, Zechariah, Malachi

Refer to the historical survey chart again and identify each prophet in his place and time.

2. *The New Testament* has basically a three–fold arrangement, determined by content:

5	21	1
HISTORY	LETTERS	PROPHECY
4 Gospels Acts	13 Pauline Epistles 8 General Epistles	Revelation
Mainly Narrative	Mainly Interpretation	Mainly Prophecy

3. *Jesus is central.* When the Old and New Testaments are viewed together as a whole, Jesus Christ becomes the key figure. The following outline illustrates:

THE KEY: JESUS

5 Books of Law	12 Historical Books	5 Poetic Books	17 Prophetic Books	4 Gospels	1 Acts	21 Letters	1 Revelation
Revel- ation	Anticipation types-experiences-prophecies			Manifes- tation	Realization		Coro- nation

This is not to say that every biblical passage is messianic or Christological, but that all Scripture, because it is the book about God and his world, focuses on the consummation of God's plans concerning this world, and Jesus Christ is the peak of that consummation (Revelation 22).

Let's take a look at the relationship between the Old and New Testaments. The two testaments are inseparable, and should be treated as one. "The New is in the Old concealed; the Old is in the New revealed." We shouldn't divide what God has joined together. The following diagram shows the intimate relationships of the two testaments.

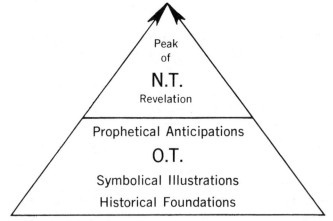

Peak
of
N.T.
Revelation

Prophetical Anticipations
O.T.
Symbolical Illustrations
Historical Foundations

The Old Testament books are the basic books of the pyramid, providing the necessary historical foundations. The Old Testament books are also picture books, filled with symbols, types, and illustrative narratives revealing the great theological truths enacted and expounded in the New. Also throughout the Old are the many prophetical anticipations of the New. Without the supernatural prophecies, the impact of future events is diminished. So the Old Testament supports, enlightens, and anticipates the New, which rises to the divine revelation of God speaking and acting through his Son (Hebrews 1:1–2), and culminates in the glorious summit where Jesus is crowned King of kings and Lord of lords.

But what about the practical side of our Bible study? If the Old Testament should be studied because it is so important, what should we look for when we are studying one of its passages?

4. *Universal subjects*. Every passage of the Bible, whether in the Old or New Testament, has something to say about one or more of the following universal subjects:

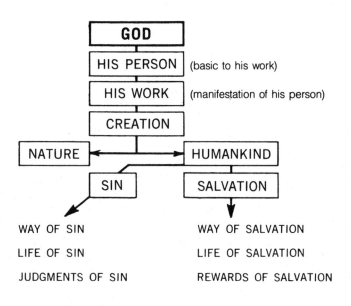

When you study an Old Testament passage, look for these truths. It's amazing how much there is to find. Salvation is the main thread woven throughout the Bible. Whether you are studying in the Old or New Testament, you will find the Bringer of Salvation, the Way of Salvation, and the People of Salvation to be the same. An Old Testament passage may illustrate a type of salvation (the deliverance of the Exodus); or graphically foretell of it (Isaiah 53); or even explicitly state it (Genesis 15:6). Whatever the mode, the revelation of godly truths should be embraced enthusiastically in both the New and the Old Testament passages.

* * *

5. *Additional Points To Remember:*

- Because the biblical writers had unique person-alities, style and vocabulary differ from book to book.

- Cultural and geographical variations occur from book to book.

- The authors' treatment of time may vary. They may skip over periods (as in prophetic "gaps"), or backtrack in descriptions (as in historical ac-counts).

- Progression in revelation is to be expected from author to author, in view of the centuries–long span of the work. No one of the writers was given a complete revelation of God's truth.

II. Approach the Bible With the Right Attitudes

The Bible is like any other book as to its literary com-position, but there the similarities end. Someone has said, "Treat the Bible like any other book, and you will find that it is not like any other book." The Bible is such a book as man could not have written if he would, and *would* not have written if he *could*. What should be our attitude toward this most unique of all books?

A. Trust
The Scriptures make fantastic claims and predictions, yet they remain completely trustworthy, because they are inspired by God. "Scripture cannot be broken" (John 10:35). The absolute Word of the absolute God is absolute authority for life. If God cannot be trusted, who can? The Bible is not a book of "cleverly invented stories," but "the word of the prophets made more certain" (2 Peter 1:16,19).

B. Dependence
We have to see our *need* of Bible study, or incentive and inspiration will be lacking. Convinced of our need to study the Bible, and knowing also our inability to understand it without help, we should depend on the Holy Spirit who indwells us (Romans 8:9) and who was given to guide us into all the truth (John 16:13). We must study the Bible under his influence, for, as D. L. Moody said, "The Bible without the Holy Spirit is a sun–dial by moonlight."

C. Reverence
The Bible is the book of the words of God. How important for us to revere its pages of truth, as it tells about the God whom we worship. Someone has said, "Access to the inmost sanctuary of the Holy Scriptures is granted only to those who come to worship." Of course we do not worship the book, but the God of the book.

Robert Evans tells of meeting an old man in bombed–out Warsaw after World War II, who had owned and cherished one page of a Bible all his life, but he was not sure that it was from the Bible. "I have read this page again and again all my life," he told Evans. "I thought it was from the Bible, but I was never sure. There is something different about it—this I know. But I have always wondered what comes on the next page." And then he wept, as Evans let him see and handle for the first time in his life an entire Bible, page by page.

D. Expectancy
The Bible is like a mine of treasures, infinitely deep, always inviting us to a second chamber, after we have spent time in the first. This was Augustine's reflection in writing his son in A.D. 412:

> Such is the depth of the Christian Scriptures that even if I were attempting to study them and nothing else from early boyhood to decrepit old age, with the utmost leisure, the most unwearied zeal, and talents greater than I have, I would still daily be making progress in discovering their treasures.

We can expect to find at least a nugget of wisdom every time we open the Bible; however, it does take an expectant attitude on our part.

E. Precision
Whether we're studying a large movement of the Bible or a small detail, we should always strive to be accurate. Because the original autographs were infallible, and because our present Bible text has been carefully preserved, it is in our best interest to study the Bible with as much care as possible. This is another attitude that honors God and produces blessed benefits.

F. Receptivity
This is the attitude of submission and "mold–ability." We approach the Bible not to do something to it, but to let it do something to us. Someone very wise once said, "Men do not reject the Bible because it contradicts itself but because it contradicts them." With an open heart and mind, we are prepared to understand the Scriptures (cf. Luke 24:45).

G. Desire
It is one thing to know that we need to study the Bible. It is another thing to desire to study it. Such a desire isn't forced, but should come naturally to the one who knows

the Author personally, and loves his fellowship. Peter had this in mind when he wrote, "Crave pure spiritual milk, so that by it you may grow up in your salvation, now that you have tasted that the Lord is good" (1 Peter 2:2–3). The book that first appeared dull to a young woman reading it suddenly became a fascinating story at a later reading, simply because in the meantime she had fallen in love with its author. The Bible is God's personal love letter to us. When we open its pages, should we regard it any less than we do a letter from our beloved?

3
How to Read
the Bible

The Bible was meant to be read. An unread Bible is like refused food, an unopened love letter, a road map not studied, a gold mine not worked. It has been aptly said that "a book is a book only when it is in the hands of a reader; the rest of the time it is an artifact." If you have put off reading your Bible, begin now to make Bible reading a vital part of your life.

Notice that this chapter is about *reading* the Bible, while the next chapter is about *studying* the Bible. Many Christians want to be Bible students without being Bible readers. Richard Moulton, a Bible scholar in his own right, made this comment:

> We have done almost everything that is possible with these Hebrew and Greek writings. We have overlaid them, clause by clause, with exhaustive commentaries; we have translated them, revised the translations, and quarrelled over the revisions; we have discussed authenticity and inspiration, and suggested textual history with the aid of colored type; we have mechanically divided the whole into chapters and verses, and sought texts to memorize and quote; we have epitomized into handbooks and extracted school lessons. . . . There is yet one thing left to do with the Bible: *simply to read it.* [1]

I. Some Practical Suggestions

The two most commonly asked questions about Bible reading are, When should I read the Bible? and, How should I read it? Of course there are no rigid answers to these questions, but there are guidelines that have proven to be successful.

A. Time

Where does one *find* time to read the Bible? Free time is so scarce for most Christians that it is never found. So we must *take* time to read the Bible, scheduling it at a regular time, if possible. Someone has said, "We ought to have a Medo–Persian hour—an unchangeable hour for our Bible study." We can easily set time aside for the daily newspaper and the weekly reading of periodicals. We should, likewise, develop the taste for daily Bible study.

The time chosen for Bible reading should be when your body and mind are fresh. Also, there should be no pressures or distractions to interfere with your being alone with God and his Word. Whatever you do, don't wait for the most *opportune* time to begin reading your Bible. Begin *now*. The biggest waste of time, in Bible study, is the time wasted in getting started.

B. Passage

The length of Scripture selection will probably vary from one time to the next, but one chapter is an average length for daily Bible study. Sometimes (especially in the deeper doctrinal portions of the Bible), you will meditate on no more than a paragraph or even a verse.

Some have chosen to read through the Bible in a year, which involves three to four chapters a day (there are 1,189 chapters in the Bible). Perhaps a more practical plan is to read through the Bible in three years (about one chapter a day). For a suggested three–year schedule, see the back of this book. Before deciding on the length of the passage to be read, remember that you want to read the selection *thoroughly*. The important thing is not how many times you've gone through the Bible, but whether the Bible has gone through *you*! George Mueller's guideline was, "I read until I come to a verse upon which I can lean my whole weight, and then stop."

In reading the Bible, it's good to alternate between the New and Old Testaments. For example, read first from the Gospels (NT); then from Genesis (OT); then dip into

. Acts or begin an Epistle (NT); then skip over to Exodus (OT), and so on. This variety keeps your study lively.

A chapter from Proverbs and Psalms could be an additional bonus to offer yourself—Proverbs offers practical advice on daily living and Psalms adds the beauty of worship to your Bible–study time. Note that there are thirty–one chapters in Proverbs, one for each day of the month.

C. Versions

Now it's time to decide which version of the Bible suits you best. Let's take a look at some of your options:

1. *One version*. Your loyalty to one version will help you in remembering Bible verses that are especially meaningful. The King James Version is a standard for memory work. Try including this version in your study session just in case you find a passage that you'd like to inscribe on your mind as well as your heart!

2. *Other versions*. You'll also benefit by reading more than one version. Modern translations are especially valuable. History shows that publication of contemporary–language Bibles results in increased sales and readership.[2] You also gain by making passage comparisons between versions. All the colors and shades of meaning are then captured by this fuller representation. Like the facets of a diamond, the many versions of the Bible add to its sparkle.

The following table represents twentieth–century renditions of the Bible:

Complete Bible:

American Standard Version . . . . (1901)
Modern Language Bible (*Berkeley Version*)(1945, 59)
Revised Standard Version . . . . (1946,* 52)
Bible in Basic English . . . .(1949)
Amplified Bible . . . . (1958, 65)
New American Standard Bible . . . . (1960)
New English Bible . . . . (1961, 70)
Good News Bible (*Today's English Version*)(1966, 76)
The Living Bible . . . . (1967, 71)

New International Version . . . . (1973, 78)
New King James Version . . . . (1979)
The Everyday Bible . . . . (1987)
(*first date denotes publication of New Testament only)

New Testament Only:

Charles B. Williams (*The New Testament
in the Language of the People*) . . . . (1937)
Charles Kingsley Williams (*The New
Testament Translation in Plain English*) . . . (1952)
J. B. Phillips (*The New Testament in
Modern English*) . . . . (1958)
Kenneth Wuest (*Expanded Translation
of the New Testament*) . . . . (1959)
William F. Beck (*The New Testament
In the Language of Today*) . . . . (1963)
William Barclay (*The New Testament*) . . . . . . (1968)

D. Editions

Versions of the Bible are printed in various editions, representing a wide spectrum of format, quality, and price. You can help your personal Bible reading immeasurably by the right choice of a Bible edition.[3] Choose an edition with large, clear print and generous space in the margins for notations. Those with the editor's marginal notes, including cross–references, are helpful, provided they stimulate personal, independent study. Paragraph format, and a text that reads across the entire page, will also enhance your reading. You'll never regret the investment you make in a good edition of the Bible.

II. What Bible Reading Really Involves

Have you ever read an entire page in a book unaware of what you were reading? If so, you know that it is possible to *read without having read!*

The eye activity of reading, basic as it is, is not enough in Bible reading. More activities are involved, which are described below under four headings: Reading, Reflection, Recording, and Response. Let's look at each of these.

A. Reading

This is the eye activity. How can we help ourselves to become keener observers, and avoid the pitfall of the heavy eye?

1. *Read aloud.* It will amaze you how new vistas are opened as you hear your own voice speaking words and sentences you may never have voiced before. Read interpretatively, with meaning and feeling. The blessed effects of reading aloud from the Psalms are described by William Law, in the classic work, *A Serious Call to the Devout and Holy Life:*

> You are to consider this [reading aloud] of a psalm as a necessary beginning of your devotions, as something that is to awaken all that is good and holy within you, that is to call your spirits to their proper duty, to set you in your best posture towards heaven, and tune all the powers of your soul to worship and adoration.
>
> For there is nothing that so clears a way for your prayers, nothing that so disperses dullness of heart, nothing that so purifies the soul from poor and careless passions, nothing that so opens heaven, or carries your heart so near to it, as these songs of praise.[4]

2. *Read Carefully.* Read alertly, not mechanically. There's a place in Bible study for the quick, cursive reading, but in devotional reading you must read slowly as well as carefully, weighing each word, noting even the punctuation. It is possible to tour a country so fast that one does not really see the land. Such a person has been called a "tripper," in contrast to the traveler, who journeys slowly to absorb not only the sights, but also the sounds and aromas. Study the Bible as a traveler not pushed by the impulse to dart off to the next stop. Gaze long across its fields of truths. Climb its mountains of vision. Cross its valleys of trial. Cool yourself in its streams of inspiration. Take in all you can as the Holy Spirit guides you through its many halls of instruction.

Train your eyes to read carefully. There is much crooked *thinking* because there is much crooked *seeing.* Each word in the Bible has a function. Always seek to learn what that function is. This may be slow going, but it is necessary. A butterfly covers more ground, but a bee gathers more honey. Be like the bee.

3. *Read Repeatedly.* Return often to the beginning of the passage. One thrust of the spade does not unearth all the gems of the mine. Don't ever conclude that you have exhausted the meaning of a verse when it becomes familiar to you. John Bunyan said that "old truths are always new to us if they come to us with the smell of heaven upon them."

4. *Read Peripherally.* Peripheral vision is seeing the surroundings while the eye is focused straight ahead. Good auto drivers and football quarterbacks must have excellent peripheral vision. So in Bible study you should keep your eyes open to the surrounding context of the words you are reading. This can be crucial in understanding the passage.

B. Reflection

When God speaks to us, we should stand still and consider what he is saying. In Bible reading, reflection is the mind and heart at work, thinking over what the eyes have seen. That's quite different from merely seeing with the eye. Reflection in Bible reading should have the intensity of meditation, with the soul yearning to obey God's Word. "Do not let this Book of the Law depart from your mouth; meditate on it day and night, so that you may be careful to do everything written in it" (Joshua 1:8).

How should we reflect on the Scriptures? Here are some suggestions:

1. *Reflect purposefully.* The psalmist had a purpose in hiding God's Word in his heart: that he might not sin against him (Psalm 119:11). The Berean Christians had a purpose in examining the Scriptures daily: that they might know the truth (Acts 17:11).

Bible meditation shouldn't be haphazard or piece-meal. If you want to keep a fire burning in your soul, don't scatter its fuel. Recall the "seed–pickers" of Paul's day who flitted here and there, picking up bits of talk about any subject, arriving at no good conclusions. (Paul was falsely accused of being a seed–picker in Acts 17:18, where the word is translated "babbler" in the *New International Version*.) Reading only isolated verses, out of context, and expanding them according to personal whims, is a dangerous practice, for, as Samuel Coleridge has said, such truths "lie bed–ridden in the dormitory of the soul, side by side with the most despised and exploded errors." It is as foolish and fruitless to read the Bible without purpose as it is to search about a room looking for nothing in particular.

What are your purposes as you meditate on the Scriptures? Do you want to know God more intimately, and glorify him? Do you want to know more about yourself? Do you want to grow strong spiritually? Do you want to know God's will, hear a word of comfort, receive a challenge? Then reflect purposefully!

2. *Reflect imaginatively.* This is not difficult, if you visualize that you are actually taking part in the scene of the Bible passage. Taste and feel every word you read. The great translator Miles Coverdale wrote to a friend, "Now I begyne to taste of Holy Schryptures; now (honour be to God) I am sett to the most swete smell of holy let-tyres."

If the passage is narrative, visualize the setting. Take this verse as an example:

> He ordered the crowd to sit down on the ground. Then he took
> the seven loaves, gave thanks to God, broke them, and gave
> them to his disciples to distribute to the crowd; and the disci-
> ples did so (Mark 8:6, TEV).

Try meditating on this verse imagining yourself as one of the crowd, or as one of the disciples.

If the passage is doctrinal or exhortative, you can still put yourself in the middle of it—after all, aren't you a pupil being taught? Try this with Colossians 2:3: "He (Christ) is the key that opens all the hidden treasures of God's wisdom and knowledge" (TEV). Imagine how rich you are in Christ!

Reflect imaginatively also on passages that no longer pertain to you—now that you are a Christian. Do you shudder when you meditate on verses like Luke 13:27–28, "I don't know you. . . . Away from me. . . . There will be weeping there, and gnashing of teeth"? Do such verses cause you to exclaim, "There am I but for the grace of God"? Do they challenge you concerning the hundreds of thousands of souls passing away daily into a Christ–less eternity? Years ago a seminary graduating class heard these words from the speaker: "Would that upon the naked, palpitating heart of each one of you might be laid one red hot coal of God Almighty's wrath!"

Something is bound to stir within your soul the moment you begin to reflect imaginatively as you read the Bible.

3. *Reflect humbly*. The words you are reading are the *holy* Word of the *holy* God. As someone has said, "Behind and beneath the Bible, above and beyond the Bible, is the God of the Bible." It should humble you to think that this Holy One, who is also the Almighty One, has spoken to you in the Bible, and has given you the blessed privilege to read it, and so to listen to him.

When you open your Bible to read it and reflect on it, remember that this is *The Holy Bible*, a title given to no other book in the world. The translators of the King James Version recognized this, as these words from their introduction testify:

The original thereof from heaven, not from earth . . .
the inditer: the Holy Spirit, not the wit of the apostles or
prophets . . .
the penmen: those that were sanctified from the womb
and endowed with a principal portion of God's Spirit . . .
the matter: verity, purity, uprightness . . .
the form: God's Word, God's testimony,
God's oracles, the Word of Truth, the Word of Salvation,
the Light of Understanding . . .
the stableness of persuasion: repentance from dead
works, newness of life, holiness, peace, and joy in the Holy
Ghost . . .
Happy is the man that delighteth in this Holy Word, and
thrice happy he that meditateth in it day and night.

4. *Reflect prayerfully.* If you reflect humbly, you will
reflect prayerfully, for the contrite heart craves to speak
to the One on whom it depends. The greatest prayer ever
prayed by a man in connection with the Scriptures is the
119th Psalm. Study this psalm carefully to learn how to
reflect prayerfully on the Word. One example is cited
here: "Open my eyes that I may see wonderful things in
your law" (Psalm 119:18).

Within that awful volume lies
The mystery of mysteries!
Happiest they of human race,
To whom God has granted grace
To read, to fear, to hope, to pray,
To lift the latch, and force the way;
And better that they'd ne'er been born,
Who read to doubt, or read to scorn.
— *Sir Walter Scott*

5. *Reflect patiently.* Patience in any area of life is priceless. The great entomologist Fabre always referred to his
best instruments as "time" and "patience." Patience on
the part of young Clyde Tombaugh is what led him finally
to discover the planet Pluto. After astronomers calcu-
lated a probable orbit for this "suspected" heavenly body
which they had never seen, Tombaugh took up the search

in March, 1929. *Time* magazine records the investigation:

> He examined scores of telescopic photographs, each showing tens of thousands of star images, in pairs under the blink comparator, or dual microscope. It often took three days to scan a single pair. It was exhausting, eye-cracking work—in his own words, "brutal tediousness." And it went on for months. Star by star, he examined twenty million images. Then on February 18, 1930, as he was blinking a pair of photographs in the constellation Gemini, "I suddenly came upon the image of Pluto!" It was the most dramatic astronomic discovery in nearly a hundred years, and it was made possible by . . . patience. [5]

The New Testament makes many references to patience. Patience is surely a requirement in the meditative process of reading God's Word. In fact the phrase "wait on the Lord" can be applied to meditation. Reflection requires time and concentration, but you'll be rewarded, as was the astronomer Tombaugh, with the pleasure and excitement of discovering stars of divine truth which you have never seen before.

The call to reflection in Bible reading is expressed in Samuel's plain words to Saul, "Stay here awhile, so that I may give you a message from God" (1 Samuel 9:27).

C. Recording

Unless you are gifted with a photographic memory, it's impossible for you to retain all the things you'll see in a productive study of a biblical passage. So what can you do to retain what you see? *Jot it down!* Put it down on a piece of paper, and also in the margins of your Bible. Underline words and phrases that strike fire in your soul. Record your observations as you see them, and your mind will be released to look for more. Professor Agassiz of Harvard said, "The pencil is one of the best eyes." Not only does recording provide a permanent record of what has been observed in Bible study; it also initiates other lines of inquiry.

Much has been written about the process of recording in the book *Independent Bible Study*.[6] Wilbur M. Smith also deals with this topic. I will quote him at length:

> We are now going to suggest something that so few Bible teachers seem to find it necessary to recommend, and yet, after years of experience, we believe it is one of the most essential aspects of personal, devotional Bible study. We refer to the making of notes. People can so easily read a page of the Bible and then give some time for meditating upon it, and actually think that they have profited by the half hour they have spent with the Word; but, if you were to ask them what they gleaned from the Word, that day, they would frequently find it difficult to put their fingers on any one rich truth that they had obtained. . . . If, however, each young Christian would have a little notebook and actually write down, morning by morning, what the Lord gives out of the verse he or she is meditating upon, it would be found that thoughts would be clarified, the profit derived from Bible study would be greatly increased, and a definite record of the things that the Holy Spirit has taught from day to day, and from week to week, would be had in permanent form. If one does not care to use a notebook, then let one use the margin of his Bible, providing it is a wide margin, and providing it will take ink . . . . The author knows of nothing that will so encourage careful reading of, and sincere meditation upon, the Word of God, delivering us from the great temptation to vagueness and indefiniteness, as a *recording* of what we have found from day to day.[7]

For your devotional reading of the Bible, here are some suggested things to record:

1. *What's the main point of the passage?* Determining such main themes is basic to understanding the various smaller parts of the passage. In this connection, choose a verse in the passage that strikes you as being a key verse. Every passage will have such a verse; some passages may yield more than one pivotal text.

2. *What do other portions of the Bible say that relate to some of these truths?* A Bible with cross–

references will help here; your acquaintance with the Bible in general will also help. For cross–reference study, a concordance will be handy.

3. *What in the passage is difficult to understand; and what problems, if any, appear?* Further reading may provide the answers. Reference to commentaries and other outside helps will aid you in a more complete analytical study.[8]

4. *How does this apply to my own life?* There are two kinds of applications involving me: vertical (God and me) and horizontal (others and me).

D. Response

All Bible study by a Christian, whether of a devotional or analytical nature, demands personal response. We are to practice what we read and reflect upon. This is the will in action. We should always be looking for examples to follow, errors to avoid, sins to confess, duties to perform, promises to claim, and prayers to echo. Let's consider three major responses which God looks for in our hearts whenever we read the Bible:

1. *Responding with confession.* Because the Bible is the Word of a holy God to people who sin, it is always searching out and exposing that sin. The Word cuts as a sword to the very inmost recesses of our being, where it "judges the desires and thoughts of man's heart. There is nothing that can be hid from God" (Hebrews 4:12, TEV). Whenever we read the Bible, it should always be with a heart that acknowledges its sin, and confesses it to God. Then the channel is cleared for further communication with God, and the blessings of Bible reading begin to accrue.

2. *Responding in faith.* Faith involves every part of our Christian life, including our Bible reading. If we do not read the Bible confidently, we lose out utterly. Hebrews 4:2 makes this very clear: "For we also have had the gospel preached to us, just as they did; but the message they heard was of no value to them, because those who heard did not combine it with faith."

3. *Responding by obedience.* When we obey God's Word, we're demonstrating where our faith rests, and how strong it is. We may not always understand God's ways, but we must always walk in his steps. A dear old woman of deep faith was chided once by an unbeliever concerning her implicit obedience to God. "I suppose if you thought the Lord was telling you to jump through a stone wall, you would jump." To that challenge her reply was simply, "If the Lord told me to jump through a wall, it would be my business to jump, and it would be his business to make the hole."

*   *   *

When you read the Bible, always be sure you are *really* reading it. Alert your eyes to see (Read); stir up your mind to consider (Reflect); write down your observations (Record); and practice what you read (Respond).

PART II
Analyzing the Bible

4
Browsing Through a Book

In the last chapter we discussed Bible *reading*. Beginning with this chapter, we'll focus on extensive, analytical *study* of the Bible. These approaches serve separate but equally important purposes. You should try to devote time to both of these methods. Devotional reading enhances your personal communion with Christ, while scriptural analysis broadens your objective understanding of the Bible text.

I. Survey Before You Analyze

Where does one begin in analytical Bible study? Experience has shown that it's best to begin by looking at the big picture first, and then progressing to the finer detail. There are two main reasons for this order of survey before analysis:

A. To grasp the overall emphasis
Remember to check for a broad understanding of the material before formulating judgments based on the detail. Prior survey is a check on the two extremes of over-emphasizing or minimizing any one point of Scripture.

B. To see the relationship between the parts
It's important to see each part in its *relation* to the other parts. Knowing one's bearing in the forest of many facts is a tremendous help in Bible study.

An experience of Charles Lindbergh illustrates this: On one of his early flights he lost a valuable instrument overboard. Later, he landed a smaller plane in the general vicinity, and scoured the area by foot in search of the instrument, but to no avail. He resorted to a simple expedient. Taking off his coat, he spread it on a bush, and returned to the air. From the air he saw both the coat and the instrument, and he made some mental notes of relationship and bearing. Landing again, he walked to the coat, but still could not find the instrument. So he moved the coat to another bush, and repeated the sighting from the air. With this additional bearing he was finally able to locate the elusive instrument.

Often, the interpretation of a verse in the Bible is based on its location within the book—the verse is better understood in reference to its context.

*   *   *

The ideal order of Bible study, then, is: a) view the entire Bible as a whole; b) choose one of the sixty–six books and survey it; and c) analyze each part (chapter or segment) of that book.

The first of these steps—surveying the whole Bible—has been discussed in chapter 2. You may want to refer to this section (pages 19-29) to review this panoramic sweep.

II. Surveying the Book of Acts

For our purposes in this chapter, we'll survey the Book of Acts. Later chapters are devoted to analytical studies of the chapter, verse, word, and topic of selected books of the Bible. Of necessity, this analysis isn't meant to be exhaustive. Instead, consider it a brief guided tour designed to encourage your independent excursions through the Bible. *Study thoroughly*, and you will *thoroughly enjoy* it!

A. Historical background
Learning the historical background of a book of the Bible is the first step of survey study. Some of this can be

learned from the text of the book itself, but you'll usually want to refer to an outside source as well.

B. Author

Read Acts 1:1, and compare it with Luke 1:1–4. From this it should be clear that Luke wrote Acts, even though his name doesn't appear in the text of Acts.

C. Date

Note from the last chapter of Acts that the final recorded event is the imprisonment of Paul in Rome. Outside sources determine this took place around A.D. 61. From all appearances, Luke wrote Acts at this time, or shortly after. Because the opening event of Acts, the ascension of Jesus, took place in A.D. 30, the book describes the first three decades of the witness of the gospel. Keep this in mind as you study Acts.

D. Function

Each book of the Bible serves a specific function among the sixty–six. A book would not be in the Bible if it didn't make its own contribution. Let's look at what Acts contributes to the New Testament:

First, observe how Acts is related to the Gospel of Luke. Read again Luke 1:1–4, then read Acts 1:1–5. Acts 1:1 says that Luke's Gospel records what Jesus *began* to do and teach, in his earthly ministry, suggesting that Acts records what he *continued* to do and teach, through the Holy Spirit. So Acts is the historical sequel to the narrative of the Gospels. In the Gospels, Christ literally gives his body as a sacrifice for men. In Acts, he begins to form his spiritual body, the church, which is comprised of all who will accept his sacrifice. The Gospels were written to record the acts of Jesus in his earthly life. Acts was written to record the church's birth and growth.

Also, Acts explains and authenticates the messages of the Epistles. For example, Paul, who wrote at least thirteen of the twenty–one Epistles, is a main character of Acts—his conversion (chapter 9) being a highlight of the book. Also, Epistles written by others (e.g., Peter and John) have their setting in the Christian communities and churches mentioned in the Book of Acts. In fact, even the seven churches of the Book of Revelation have their origins in Acts. So Acts is a pivotal book in the New Testament.

Additionally, Acts serves to vindicate the stand of the new Christian community amid persecution stemming from false charges both religious and political.

III. The Survey Process

Don't be tempted to take shortcuts in Bible study. If you seek one, you're likely to miss some treasures along the avoided paths. In your personal study of the Bible, don't become impatient or discouraged by slow progress. If you are diligently reading the text and letting it soak into your heart and mind, you can claim the promise of Isaiah 55:10–11:

> As the rain and the snow come down from heaven, and do not return to it without watering the earth and making it bud and flourish, so that it yields seed for the sower and bread for the eater, so is my word that goes out from my mouth: It will not return to me empty, but will accomplish what I desire and achieve the purpose for which I sent it.

Aim at making steady progress in Bible study, and don't worry about the speed of travel. Every small gain offers you greater wisdom and understanding. Let the progression be from first impressions, to repeated impressions, to enduring impressions; or from the random and indefinite, to the organized and defined. The important element is perseverance—*read and read and read!*

A. First reading

Initially, we'll want to take a quick, first impression. Rather than reading slowly through any one chapter, our first exercise will be to read through the twenty–eight chapters of Acts in one sitting, if possible. We'll call this "browsing through the book." This is to get the "feel" of the book, and to see the highlights from the start. Don't be tempted to linger over particular passages at this point. The key is to read it as one narrative, overlooking even the chapter divisions. Don't try to discover organization. Strictly skim through this first reading. For this, it's helpful to read from an everyday–language version, such as *The Everyday Bible*.

What are your first impressions after this first reading? They might include

- the opposition by enemies of the gospel (e.g., chapters 3–7);

- the faith and courage of early Christians (e.g., chapter 7);

- the triumph of the church (e.g., 4:18–23)

- the many miracles (e.g., 7:8);

- the advance of the gospel geographically and nationally (e.g., 13:3ff.);

- the prominent part of the Holy Spirit in the narrative;

- the many sermons in the early part of Acts (e.g., 2:14ff.), and the defenses advanced by Paul (one in each of chapters 22–26); and

- the many travels by Paul to reach new cities with the gospel (chapters 13–21).

Just one reading of Acts is an inspiration in itself. But we must go on to more, for we've just begun to draw upon its storehouse of wisdom.

B. Second reading

In our first reading we didn't try to discover the organization of the book. Now, however, we want to begin to see Luke's plan. Luke, like all writers, selected what to include in his work, and what to omit. He brought his materials together according to a plan, and the wonderful Book of Acts was produced. Luke did all this under the inspiration of the Holy Spirit, which gave the book not only veracity but also spiritual depth and beauty. Let's look for clues to the organization of the book, and begin to record these on a survey chart. When we've seen the plan and outline of the Book of Acts, we begin to understand more about the power behind the first–century church, and the overall design of a wise and sovereign God.

1. *Chapter titles.* First, assign titles to each chapter (or segment, if the unit is shorter or longer than a chapter). This helps us to fix in our minds something of the "flow" of the book.[1] Record the titles on a horizontal chart as follows:

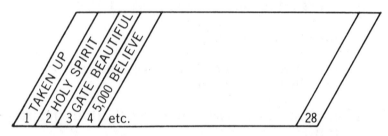

Sometimes a unit of study doesn't begin with the first verse of the chapter. Normally, though, it's best to proceed as though there were no such exceptions, and pick these up at a later time, when they usually show themselves. We'll anticipate this step now, by identifying the exceptions for Acts:

Units of study in Acts which begin in the middle of a chapter:

9:32 (in addition to 9:1);
15:36 (instead of 16:1);
18:23 (instead of 19:1);
21:18 (in addition to 21:1).

2. *Emphasis by repetition.* If a particular theme is repeated often, we may safely assume it is central to the organization of the book. Let's look at some of the more important *repeated* items in Acts.

a) *miracles:* Miracles appear throughout Acts (see 28:5–6), validating the supernatural message of the apostles to a new group or situation.

b) *witness:* The word "witness" is a key word of Acts. Referring to an exhaustive concordance[2], we find that it appears twenty–one times. A key verse for Acts is 1:8:

> But you will receive power when the Holy Spirit comes on you;
> and you will be my witnesses in Jerusalem, and in all Judea
> and Samaria, and to the ends of the earth.

The idea of witness itself gives no clue as to any divisions in the organization of Acts, for the Christians continue to witness throughout the book. But the geography of that witness is a definite clue, clearly showing three areas of witness, fulfilled in the order of Jesus' prophecy: 1) *Jerusalem*, 2) *Judea and Samaria*, and 3) *the ends of the earth*. Notice that Jerusalem is the center of the witness of chapters 1–7; at 8:1b the church, excluding the apostles, "were scattered throughout Judea and Samaria"; and 13:1 begins the first thrust of the witness of the gospel to "foreign" lands, the "uttermost" parts of the Roman Empire. So we make this geographical outline of "witness" for our survey chart of Acts:

1	8:1b	13:1 28
JERUSALEM	JUDEA & SAMARIA	UTTERMOST PARTS

As we proceed in our study, we will observe that the three divisions noted above are the three main parts of Acts with respect to other topics as well.

c) *Jew, Gentile:* Acts refers often to the Jews (mainly under the name Israel) and Gentiles. A comparative study in an exhaustive concordance will show that references to Israel appear mostly in the first part of the book, while the Gentiles appear mostly after chapter 8. This is because the church in Acts is shown to move from a constituency mainly of Jews to one that included Gentiles as well. Chapters 10 and 11 are the key chapters pointing to this transition. It might be helpful to read these chapters again. At 13:1, where Paul's missionary party begins its evangelistic invasion of cities throughout the Roman Empire, the gospel is presented as a universal gospel. This study can be shown on a chart (note that we are using the junctions 8:1b and 13:1 which appeared in our study on "witness"):

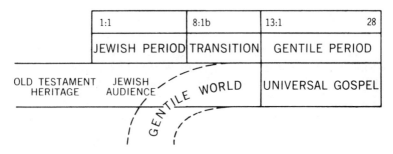

1:1	8:1b	13:1 28
JEWISH PERIOD	TRANSITION	GENTILE PERIOD
OLD TESTAMENT HERITAGE JEWISH AUDIENCE	GENTILE WORLD	UNIVERSAL GOSPEL

d) *Peter, Paul:* The study of *persons* in any historical book of the Bible will often give clues to the organization of the book. In Acts, Peter is definitely *the* leading apostle of chapters 1–7, while Paul is the leading person of chapters 13–28. In the transitional section, chapters 8–12, the four main people are Peter, Philip, Barnabas, and Paul, with Peter still the most active. We should record this on our survey chart also.

1	8:1b	13:1 28
PETER	Philip-Barnabas Peter-Paul	PAUL
ACTS OF PETER		ACTS OF PAUL

e) *the church:* This is another key subject of Acts, the word itself appearing twenty–two times in the book. The church is the agent used by God to bear witness to the gospel. An extensive title for Acts might be, *The Gospel in Action by the Holy Spirit Through the Church.* Following the three-fold outline of Acts given in the above descriptions, Acts shows:

the church established (1–7);
the church scattered (8–12);
the church extended (13–28).

The church was born on Pentecost, when the disciples were gathered in Jerusalem (1:12; 2:1). When the Book of Acts ends, there is a group of believers, part of the universal church, living in Rome (28:24). This extension of the church from east (Jerusalem) to west (Rome) is a fascinating story. To give it more attention in survey study, one would have to read through Acts another time, concentrating on how the subject of the church is developed chapter by chapter.

*　　*　　*

Although the main purpose of surveying a Bible book is orientation, we shouldn't ignore personal applications. For instance, a comparison of the beginning and ending of Acts suggests an important spiritual lesson. What Jesus had commissioned and prophesied at the opening of Acts, "You will be my witnesses" (1:8), was being accomplished faithfully and unhindered at the end of Acts—"taught about the Lord Jesus Christ" (28:31). Now, let's ask ourselves the question, Did the Acts of the Holy Spirit end with the Book of Acts? A thousand times no! There is something about the ending of Acts that suggests an unfinished, continuing symphony. The last word in the Greek text is akolutos, meaning "unhindered" (translated in the King James Version by four words, "no man forbidding him"). It is as though there is no period at the end of the sentence: Paul would keep on witnessing, and the other Christians would keep on witnessing, and generations after them would keep on witnessing. *And we today should keep on witnessing!*

*　　*　　*

You've just read the Book of Acts more than once. Do you suppose that you've learned all there is to learn? John Morley wrote: "It is a great mistake to think that because you have read a masterpiece once or twice or ten times, therefore you have done with it. Because it is a masterpiece you ought to live with it, and make it a part of your daily life." A survey study of a Bible book serves only to invite more thrilling discoveries.

After you've finished a survey study of a book, the next series of studies should be an analysis of each chapter of that book. With the acquaintance you now have with the highlights of Acts, you can see that such a panoramic view of the book will help in your more detailed study of the smaller parts.[3] In the next chapters we'll look at ways to analyze smaller parts of the Bible. For variety, we'll turn to the Old Testament for our analysis.

Suggested Exercises

Using Acts as an example, you've learned in this chapter how to survey a Bible book. Why not try surveying another Bible book on your own? Use Exodus as the book for this survey. A minimal set of directions is given below. Record observations on a survey chart whenever possible.

1. Scan the book once or twice for such things as: tone, large movements, turning points, emphases, comparisons, and contrasts.

2. Record chapter titles on a survey chart.

3. Contrast the first and last chapters of Exodus. What is the state of Israel in each chapter?

4. Make a list of the major *events* and *characters* of Exodus. Record these on the chart.

5. What is the general geographical movement of Exodus?

6. Compare the general content of the first half of Exodus (1–18) with that of the last half (19–40).

7. What is the main difference between the content of chapters 25–31 and that of chapters 35–40?

8. Name three major truths about God that are prominent in the text of Exodus.

9. Make some outlines for Exodus on such topics as: geography, experiences of Israel, revelation of God.

10. In your own words, what is the theme of Exodus?

11. Try to choose a key verse for Exodus; also identify some key words expressive of the theme of the book.

5
Charting a Chapter

Chapter study is perhaps the most common of all Bible studies. In this chapter we'll discuss ways to chart our observations on an analytical chart.

This analysis will begin with Joshua 5, purposely selected to increase your confidence in studying from the Old Testament. Many Christians consider the Old Testament dry, out of date, and too difficult to comprehend, but it is actually full of thrilling stories, written in the concrete language of the five senses. True, at places there are long lists of genealogy, geography, and other necessary citations, but these obstacles aren't insurmountable.

When the Bible was first divided into chapter units, practical considerations were probably foremost in mind. An average chapter's length (about twenty–six verses) is a reasonable study unit, and the area of focus is workable.

Sometimes a chapter division could have been more favorably located (e.g., chapter 53 of Isaiah could begin with the verse 52:13), but most of the Bible's chapters begin with a new unit of thought. On occasion, we may choose to identify a passage for analysis to include more or less than a chapter, providing it is still a unit of thought. These passages could be called segments, since the word "chapter" wouldn't rightly apply. Although the passage we're studying (Joshua 5:2–15) isn't a full chapter,[1] we'll refer to it as a chapter, for the sake of simplicity.

I. The Process of Analysis

Survey study, which was our exercise in Acts, scans

the surface, looking for the high points. Analysis study probes a limited area, clarifying implication and suggestion. Follow this suggested order in your analysis:

Observe—What does the passage say?

Interpret—What does the passage mean?

Apply—How does this apply to today?

Each of these areas will be explained in turn later. A word might be said here about using outside helps in Bible study. The key to constructive study habits is to resort to these mainly toward the *end of our personal study.* The temptation comes to consult a commentary prematurely. Discipline yourself to mainly concentrate on the Bible passage. Good outside helps are intended to serve the student as spades, not crutches. There's no rival to the excitement of *first–hand* discoveries of biblical treasure.

A. Observation

1. *Orientation of context.* There is one exception to the rule of avoiding Bible commentaries early in your study. This is in determining the chapter's setting in the large movement of the book. Usually, chapter study is pursued consecutively, with survey of the whole book first (such as we did for Acts in the last chapter), followed by studies in chapter 1, chapter 2, and so forth. When one studies an isolated chapter in the Bible, however, it is very important to become acquainted with that chapter's context. Dip into a Bible commentary just to learn the setting. For this purpose it is a practical source of help.

The rule of context calls for a consideration of *the whole revelation* of the truth being taught. This applies to both the overall context and the immediate context.

A familiar illustration of the latter is a story about the Battle of Waterloo. All England was waiting to receive the news as to the outcome of the battle. Communication was by signal lights from station to station. One of these was located on top of Winchester Cathedral. At a late hour of the day the message was received: *"Wellington . . . Defeated. . . ."* Just at that moment a fog descended, and the report of Wellington's disaster was spread throughout London. But when the fog suddenly lifted again, it was seen that there was more to the message. *The full report* was: *"Wellington Defeated the Enemy."* In Bible study we should always consider the whole revelation of the truth being taught.

2. *Survey of the context of Joshua.* In surveying Joshua, we learn that the book is about Israel taking possession of the Promised Land of Canaan. In Exodus, Israel began its migration from Egypt to Canaan. In Leviticus, the nation was given laws to live by, especially for their life in the new land. Numbers narrates their journey (and temporary delay by judgment) in the Sinai wilderness. Deuteronomy records the preparations made as the people were waiting to enter Canaan under the leadership of Moses' successor, Joshua.

Joshua is the story of *taking the inheritance*, an inheritance promised by God. The phrase epitomizing the book is, "So Joshua took the whole land" (11:23a). The story is told in four parts:

- Preparation (chapters 1–5);

- Conquest (chapters 6–12);

- Division of Inheritance (chapters 13–21); and

- Consecration (chapters 22–24).

The first half of the book (1–12) is filled with *action*, while the second half describes both the *business* of listing inheritances (13–21), and the *exhortations* to the people, as they anticipate dwelling in the new land. (See the diagram on the next page).

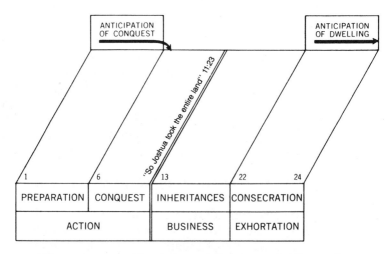

- **The *preparation*** stage (chapters 1–5) involves the Israelites mobilization and reconnaissance (chapters 1–2); getting into position by crossing the Jordan (3:1–5:1); and spiritual renewal (5:2–15). This last preparation is the object of our present analytical study. When the Israelites fulfilled these spiritual exercises, they were ready to launch out in their campaigns for conquest. Crossing the Jordan brought the nation into geographical position; now they needed to be brought into spiritual position.

- **Joshua's strategy for *conquest*** (chapters 6–12) called for three campaigns: 1) central, involving the key cities of Jericho and Ai (6:1–8:35); 2) southern (9:1–10:43); and 3) northern (11:1–15). The passage 11:16–12:24 is a summary of Joshua's conquests.

- **The business of assigning *inheritances*** (chapters 13–21) called for special allotments (chapters 13–14), and major allotments and special provisions (chapters 15–21).

- **The book ends on the high peak of *consecration*** (chapters 22–24), centered about the altar of witness (chapter 22) and a renewal of the covenant which God had originally made with Abraham (chapters 23–24).

With this survey of Joshua in mind, we are given a perspective for chapter 5. Note on the chart opposite where chapter 5 appears. This chapter of spiritual preparation was a vital and necessary exercise for the Israelites, if they were to expect victory in their battles with the enemies. If they did not defeat Satan in their own personal lives and in the life of the nation, they could not expect to drive out the enemies from the land which God had promised them. For the project of possessing Canaan was more than a military venture; it was the entrance into a new life, in God's "rest–land," with God as the Lord of their lives. The Book of Hebrews, chapters 3 and 4, interprets for us what this "rest–land" living involved. For the Israelites already in covenant relationship with God, it demanded continued faith and obedience, and offered all the blessings of partaking in the life of God. The possessing of Canaan was an Old Testament type, not of a man becoming saved, but of one, already saved, appropriating all the fullness of the blessings of Christ's Lordship, as "partakers of Christ" (Hebrews 3:14; cf. 4:11).

As we study Joshua 5:2–15, therefore, let's look for truths as they bear upon your own Christian life, particularly the victorious life in the fullness of Christ, which is Christian "rest–land" living.

*   *   *

JOSHUA 5:2-15

2

10

11

13

15

For best results, we should be methodical in recording our studies. Here's a simple method: block out a rectangle (about 4" x 9") on a sheet of paper (8 1/2" x 11"). For Joshua 5:2–15, block off four paragraphs, beginning at verses 2, 10, 11, and 13. (At the outset of chapter study, identify the paragraphs. We may follow the suggested divisions of our Bible versions, or determine our own.) Our worksheet should look something like the chart opposite. Having definite areas on the worksheet encourages orderliness and purpose in our notes. This is a visual aid that will prove valuable in all our analytical studies.

3. *Observations of Joshua 5:2–15*. Observe accurately and completely and you'll be well on the path to correct interpretation. Sharp observation is so important to valid interpretation that it will be stressed as we study Joshua 5. After we have read this passage a few times, we should begin to record things. Some suggestions follow, which are applicable to any segment of study:

a) *first impressions:* It is impressive to read, for example, that God commanded the Israelites to take the time and energy necessary to observe such ceremonies as circumcision or Passover, on the eve of battle. Might not these have been postponed until after battle? Obviously the lesson was: spiritual preparation *must be given top priority* for all engagements. Also, we are reminded in this passage how much the Old Testament is filled with the picturesque and the active. God revealed theological truths in concrete, dynamic forms, rather than abstractly. Read Joshua 5, and make a note of your own first impressions.

b) *atmosphere, repetitions and other laws of composition:* The atmosphere of the words of these verses changes from plain observance of holy ceremonies (2–12) to awesome respect of holy ground (13–15). As for repetitions, the word "circumcise" is the key word of the first paragraph, and should, therefore, be a clue to the paragraph's main purpose. Contrast, progression, turning–

point and centrality are other structural characteristics looked for in any chapter.

B. Interpretation and application.

1. *Questions for discovery.* These indispensable study tools Rudyard Kipling has called his "serving–men":

> I keep six honest serving–men
> (They taught me all I knew);
> Their names are What and Why and When
> And How and Where and Who
> I send them over land and sea,
> I send them east and west;
> But after they have worked for me,
> I give them all a rest.

Now apply these tools to the text:

*   *What:* What is the prominent object or action in each paragraph? The answers are clear:

    First paragraph (2–9):   circumcision

    Second paragraph (10):   passover

    Third paragraph (11–12):   fruit

    Fourth paragraph (13–15):   sword

This leads to an associated question: What is each of these a token of?

circumcision	—token of covenant (Notes in the Bible or a concordance will direct us to Genesis 17:9–14 for this answer.)
passover blood	—token of atonement (shown by Exodus 12:1–20)

fruit   —token of feasting (not the provisional manna, Exodus 16:15)

sword   —token of victories

In the life of a believer, covenant and atonement have to do with position—"**life**"; feasting and victories have to do with experience—"**living**." As we record these on the worksheet, we begin to anticipate some spiritual applications involving Christians:

- *Where:* Notice places in the passage.

First paragraph: Egypt, Gilgal

Second paragraph: plains of Jericho

Third paragraph: Canaan

Fourth paragraph: "place . . . holy"

Are any spiritual truths suggested by the places, in view of Israel's past or present experiences? Here are some observations and conclusions:

1 COVENANT —circumcision	2	**LIFE** (position)
2 ATONEMENT —blood	10	
3 FEASTING —fruit	11	**LIVING** (experience)
4 VICTORIES —sword	13	
	15	

Restoration:	Reproach of Egypt rolled away (Gilgal: literally, "circle") See Exodus 32:12.
Deliverance assured:	In the face of the enemy, on the plains of Jericho.
Provision enjoyed:	Canaan, a gift of God.
Sanctification:	The presence of God, in the holy place.

- **Who** is the main person of the narrative?
  See how each paragraph shows who this is:

Circumcision:	God had initiated the covenant between himself and Israel (Genesis 17:9–14), and now renews it (Joshua 5:2–9).
Passover blood:	The key phrase of this rite was always, "When I see the blood, I will pass over you" (Exodus 12:13). The Passover ceremony was originally commanded by God to be an annual event (Exodus 12:14). Up until this time the Israelites had observed it only once (Numbers 9:5) since the original event. Now was the time of renewal, to obey God's command again.
Fruit:	The manna ceased at God's bidding, and he gave the new "produce of Canaan" (Joshua 5:12).
Sword:	God would fight Israel's battles, through his "commander" (Joshua 5:14).

So the experiences of Israel during this time of spiritual preparation not only reminded them of the prominent place of God in their lives, but also that their God was a gracious, *giving* God, showering his gifts on his undeserving people. When we read into the next chapter, this is reiterated at 6:2 concerning the land itself: "See, I have *delivered* Jericho into your hands. . . ."

Everything good that we as Christians have is a gift from God. Do we acknowledge this, and thank him continually?

- **When:** There is a time reference involving each paragraph.

PAST:

Circumcision:	renewing the covenant made earlier with Abraham
Passover:	recalling the great Passover deliverance of the exodus

PRESENT AND FUTURE:

Fruit:	the new diet, advancing from manna to various foods of the field and vine
Sword:	assurance of victory in the battles to come

We as Christians look back to our experience of salvation, when we first began our life of covenant relationship to God, when we were delivered from the bondage of sin by the shed blood of Christ. Having been saved, we now can enter into the fullness of joy which comes as we experience the wonderful varieties of spiritual food from heaven, and receive the blessings of victories in battle with Satan, by the power of Christ.

- *How and Why:* These kinds of questions may open doors to the deepest of truths in a passage. For example:

HOW is shed blood acceptable to God for the remission of sins?

HOW did God speak to Joshua and other saints of old?

WHY did God's commander call that place "holy"?

2. *A main outline for the passage.* Now that we've studied the passage, we may begin to organize an outline. Because this should reflect the main theme and determine a key verse, state these first:

a) *main theme:* For appropriating God's rest–land, there needs to be spiritual renewal of fellowship with God, recognition of his atoning work, a foretaste of blessings to come, and a total dependence on him for victory.

b) *key verse:* "the land that he had solemnly promised their fathers to give us, a land flowing with milk and honey" (5:6b).

Now for an outline, based on the theme. There are various ways of wording this—the more simply stated, the better. (See the analytical chart on page 72.)

A main title: BLESSINGS OF SPIRITUAL REST

Main paragraph points: *1. Covenant*
(one per paragraph)   *2. Atonement*
                    3. Feasting
                    4. Victories

If we had worded the title *Tokens of Spiritual Rest,* the tokens themselves would have been the paragraph points: 1) circumcision, 2) blood, 3) fruit, 4) sword.

c) *subordinate points in each paragraph:* Here we observe the items in each paragraph that support the main point of that paragraph. Look for these, and record them on your worksheet. Notice how we derive a spiritual lesson from a historical illustration. Care must be exercised here to avoid extreme spiritualization; nevertheless, we need to be alert to the suggestion of historical facts in terms of spiritual application.

BLESSINGS OF SPIRITUAL REST

I. Covenant (verses 2–9)

   A. A relationship desired by God (implied in the passage)

   B. A relationship demanding obedience (verse 6)

   C. A relationship that dispels reproach (verse 9)

II. Atonement (verse 10)

   A. Affords a dwellingplace ("camped")

   B. Gives assurance of sins forgiven ("Passover"; "I will pass over you")

   C. Defies the enemy ("on the plains of Jericho")

III. Feasting (verses 11–12)

   A. Bleak survival ceases ("the manna stopped"—verse 12)

   B. Bountiful living begins ("ate of the produce of Canaan"—verse 12)

IV. Victories

   A. The foe is real (verse 13)

   B. The issue is holy (verse 15)

   C. The victory is the Lord's (verse 14)

BLESSINGS OF SPIRITUAL REST

Tokens:

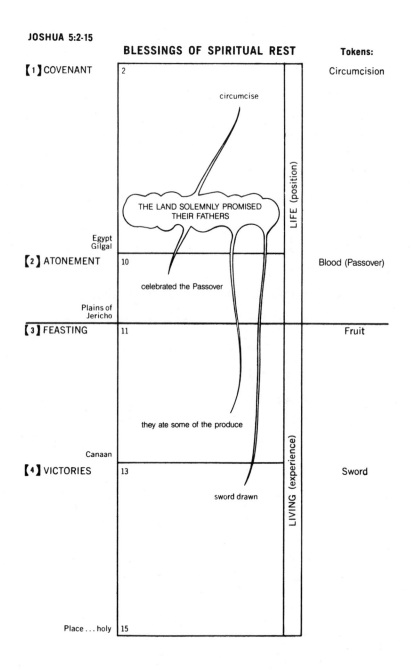

【1】 COVENANT — Circumcision

circumcise

THE LAND SOLEMNLY PROMISED THEIR FATHERS

LIFE (position)

Egypt
Gilgal

【2】 ATONEMENT — Blood (Passover)

celebrated the Passover

Plains of
Jericho

【3】 FEASTING — Fruit

they ate some of the produce

LIVING (experience)

Canaan

【4】 VICTORIES — Sword

sword drawn

Place ... holy

3. *Words and phrases for further study.* For this passage such words might be "Passover," "holy," "are you for us?" Suggestions for word study are given later in this book.

4. *Problem passages.* If our analysis fails to find answers to problem passages, we should consult a commentary for help.[2] We will want to use commentaries as supplementary aids as well, *after* our independent study.

Interpretations and applications are dependent on observations, but they may be made along the way in your study, as we have done in this study. Applications should always be made in the spirit and intent of the Bible passage. Interpretation out of context is illustrated by the farmer who went out to the fields to work and encouraged his laziness by recalling Philippians 4:5, KJV: "Let your moderation be known unto all men"; then he continued in the folly of his faulty application when he sat down to the dinner table at night with Ecclesiastes 9:10, "Whatever your hand finds to do, do it with all your might."

The New Testament is of inestimable value for interpreting the Old Testament. Look at Hebrews 3 and 4 again, chapters which give the Christian meaning to the Israelites' rest–land living. There we discover some of the blessings of the victorious life. It is interesting to observe how many of these are taught, some by allusion, in the Joshua passage which we have been studying. Included are:

- Sharing in a heavenly calling (Hebrews 3:1)

- Fellowship with Christ, in his house. In fact, we *are* his house (3:6)

- Fruits of faith (4:1–10)

- The Word of God at work (4:12–13)

- Intercession of Jesus as our high priest (4:14–15)

- Access to the throne of grace (4:16)

- Help in time of need (4:16)

If these are blessings, what are the demands on us? From Hebrews the main commands are:

- Hold firmly our courage and faith (3:6; 4:14)

- Believe (3:12) and obey (3:18—"those who disobeyed")

- Approach boldly the throne of grace with confidence (4:16)

II. A Partial List of Key Chapters in the Bible

The following chapters are ideal for further independent study.

OLD TESTAMENT	NEW TESTAMENT
Genesis 3	Matthew 5–7
—Fall	—Beatitudes
Genesis 7	Matthew 13
—Flood	—Parables
Genesis 22	Matthew 25
—Sacrifice	—Judgment
Exodus 12	Mark 10
—Passover	—Eternal Life
Exodus 20	Luke 10
—Law	—Service
Exodus 32	Luke 15
—Idolatry	—The Lost
Leviticus 16	John 1
—Sin offering	—Divinity
Leviticus 23	John 3
—Day of Atonement	—Regeneration

Deuteronomy 32
—Song of Moses
Joshua 1
—Challenge
Ruth 1
—Constancy
1 Samuel 7
—Conquest
1 Samuel 15
—Disobedience
1 Samuel 20
—Friendship
2 Kings 5
—Leprosy Cured
Nehemiah 4
—Builders
Psalm 1
—The Two Ways
Psalm 23
—Shepherd
Psalm 32
—Converts
Psalm 39
—Frailty
Psalm 51
—Confession
Psalm 73
—Prosperity
Psalm 91
—Safety
Proverbs 1
—Instruction
Proverbs 23
—Temperance
Ecclesiastes 12
—Old Age
Isaiah 6
—Worker's Call
Isaiah 52:13–53:12
—Messiah

John 6
—Bread of Life
John 10
—Shepherd
John 11
—Lazarus
John 13
—Humility
John 15
—Fruit
John 17
—Intercession
Acts 1
—Ascension/Commission
Acts 12
—Deliverance
Romans 1
—Universal Condemnation
Romans 6
—Victory
Romans 8
—Holy Spirit
Romans 12
—Duty
1 Corinthians 2
—True Wisdom
1 Corinthians 12
—Gifts
1 Corinthians 13
—Love
1 Corinthians 15
—Resurrection
Ephesians 2
—Grace
Ephesians 6
—Soldier
Philippians 2
—Humility
Colossians 3
—Heavenly Mind

Isaiah 55
—Universal Call
Daniel 6
—Prayer
Hosea 14
—Backsliding
Jonah 2
—Deliverance

1 Thessalonians 5
—Second Coming
2 Timothy 2
—A Good Minister
Hebrews 1:1–2:4
—Supreme Revelation
Hebrews 4
—Rest
Hebrews 11
—Faith
James 3
—Tongue
2 Peter 1
—Abundant Life
1 John 1
—Walk
Revelation 2–3
—Overcomers
Revelation 22
—Heaven

Suggested Exercises

Analyze Isaiah 6:1–13, recording your observations and outlines on an analytical chart. Make paragraph divisions at verses 1, 5, 8, and 11.

1. Read the chapter once or twice for initial impressions and other observations. As you read try to picture the scene and the action, and try to hear the voices of the speakers. Record paragraph titles.

2. Where in the chapter does Isaiah's call actually begin?

3. What is the main point of each paragraph? Who is the main person of the first paragraph? Of the second paragraph? Who asks the question

4. What is the atmosphere of each of the first two paragraphs?

5. Compare the beginning and end of the chapter.

6. Analyze verses 1–4. Who is the central person, and how is he shown to be central? Study carefully the ascription of verse 3.

7. Analyze verses 5–7. Account for Isaiah's reaction. How does Isaiah identify himself? How does he identify God? What is the purging agent of verses 6–7?

8. Analyze verses 8–10. Observe this outline: Call; Response; Commission. For help in interpreting verses 9–10, read Matthew 13:13–17.

9. Analyze verses 11–13. Observe the two–fold message of judgment and salvation. Note the opening words of verse 13: "And though."

10. Write out some lessons taught by this chapter about: divine call; Lord's glory; confession of sin; Christian service; hardened hearts; grace of God.

6
Probing a Paragraph

The original writers of the books of the Bible did not divide their books into chapters, paragraphs or verses—to do so would have left blank spaces on the pages of the manuscript, a prohibitive extravagance in view of the high cost of parchment. In fact, there was no space between words and sentences! It was up to the reader to figure out the author's structure. And the authors did follow certain plans in writing, even though these did not appear in the format of the manuscripts. They added unit to unit (our chapters), developing each unit by a series of smaller units (our paragraphs). All Bibles published today use a standard set of chapter and verse divisions, but differ as to paragraph divisions.

I. The Paragraph

When a chapter of the Bible is being analyzed, a full analysis of each paragraph must be made, because the paragraphs make the chapter. In chapter 5 we studied the passage Joshua 5:2–15, including its four paragraphs. Because no one paragraph was singled out in that study, this chapter will focus on one paragraph, and suggest a method of analysis. This is what we call *probing a paragraph.*

The paragraph to analyze is 1 John 1:1–4. It will help to first glance at its context, which includes a little more than the chapter. The study unit is 1:1–2:6. Diagrammed on a worksheet such as we used earlier, the skeleton of this segment might look something like the chart on page 81.

Now carefully examine the first paragraph of this segment, verses 1–4. Just as a scientist lays out his specimen on the laboratory table to make a complete, unbiased examination of each part and of the interrelationship of the parts, so we approach this paragraph. A good way to "lay out" the paragraph before us is to print its verses in a box as shown, a procedure called textual re–creation. The purpose of textual re–creation is to *pictorialize* the biblical text showing in visual form not only *what* the text is saying, but *how* it is saying it. Repetitions, comparisons, and progressions are some of the things which we can picture by such writing devices as indentation, underlinings, arrows, and so forth. An example of a simple textual re–creation of this paragraph, with a brief outline placed in the margin, is shown on page 82.

Of course, to make a textual re–creation of a paragraph demands that we see things before we record. This is the whole point of analysis in scientific examination. We observe first, record the observations, compare the findings, and reach conclusions.

Remember, in observation we are studying in two areas: 1) what each part says, and 2) how all the parts are related. Many Bible students stop with the first area, and forfeit all the enlightenment offered by the second area.

Observe some of the things that paragraph, 1 John 1:1–4, is telling us.

1 JOHN 1:1—2:6

POSSIBLE THROUGH

HEAVENLY FELLOWSHIP

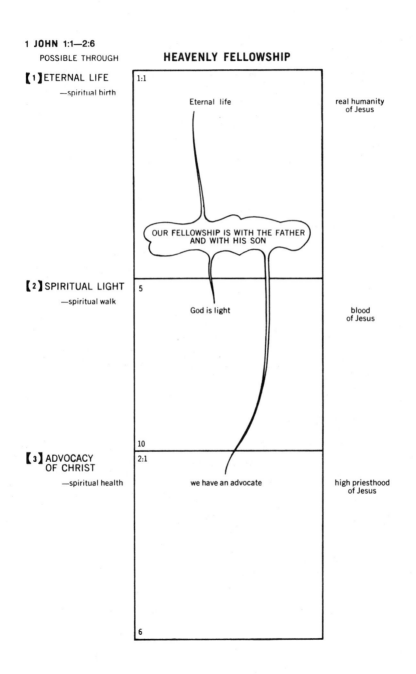

【1】ETERNAL LIFE

—spiritual birth

1:1

Eternal life

real humanity
of Jesus

OUR FELLOWSHIP IS WITH THE FATHER
AND WITH HIS SON

【2】SPIRITUAL LIGHT

—spiritual walk

5

God is light

blood
of Jesus

10

【3】ADVOCACY
OF CHRIST

—spiritual health

2:1

we have an advocate

high priesthood
of Jesus

6

1 JOHN 1:1-4

TEXTUAL RE-CREATION

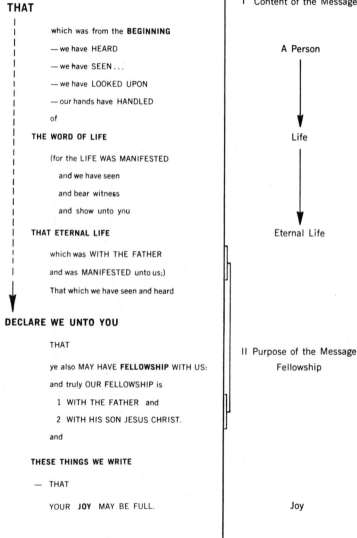

WE DECLARE <u>THAT</u>!

I Content of the Message

THAT

    which was from the **BEGINNING**

    — we have HEARD

    — we have SEEN . . .

    — we have LOOKED UPON

    — our hands have HANDLED

    of

THE WORD OF LIFE

    (for the LIFE WAS MANIFESTED

      and we have seen

      and bear witness

      and show unto you

THAT ETERNAL LIFE

    which was WITH THE FATHER

    and was MANIFESTED unto us;)

    That which we have seen and heard

DECLARE WE UNTO YOU

    THAT

    ye also MAY HAVE **FELLOWSHIP** WITH US:

    and truly OUR FELLOWSHIP is

      1 WITH THE FATHER and

      2 WITH HIS SON JESUS CHRIST.

    and

THESE THINGS WE WRITE

    — THAT

    YOUR **JOY** MAY BE FULL.

A Person

Life

Eternal Life

II Purpose of the Message
    Fellowship

Joy

4

A. The core of a long sentence

In the King James Version, the first three verses are one sentence. What is the core of the sentence? That is, what is the main subject, main verb, and main object?

> main subject: "we"
>
> main verb: "declare"
>
> main object: "that"
>
> indirect object: "unto you"

John has hidden his main point in the grammatical structure of the sentence, because he wanted to focus attention on a description of the "that" (the message of the gospel), which was really the Person, Jesus Christ.

"We declare unto you." Stated another way, in exclamatory fashion, "This we declare!" This is the main theme of the paragraph, a study developed further in the right-hand column of the chart opposite.

When we place each phrase of the sentence in its proper relationship to the core, the passage begins to unfold. We note that the first half of the paragraph describes the content of the message, while the last half tells the purpose of declaring the message.

B. Observations

Looking more closely at the first half, we'll describe the content of the message:

1. *Progression.* The message is really a person, and obviously, from the descriptions ("we have heard . . . seen . . . handled") the person is Jesus. But not named as such, he is, instead, associated with *Life*. But what kind of life? Life lived unto himself? Or a life-giving life? The latter; in fact, his life imparts 'eternal life' to others. So there is a progression in the description, shown in the sequence: Person→Life→Eternal Life. Other won-

derful thoughts are suggested by phrases in the text. These are just some suggestions.

2. *Repetition.* We should always look for repetitions in the Bible. Repetitions are usually easy to detect, and furnish one of the best clues to the intent of a passage. In this paragraph, two key repeated words are 'life' and 'fellowship.' But notice another important repetition: two clauses of purposes beginning with the word 'that' (meaning 'in order that'). John cites two purposes for declaring the gospel of Jesus: 1) "that ye . . . may have fellowship with us" (verse 3), and 2) "that your [our][1] joy may be full."

3. *Time references.* When we look for references to 'when' in this passage, two explicit ones appear: 'beginning' and 'eternal.' Jesus was not created, but was existing when the creation began. In fact he existed from all eternity past, for he was "with the Father." And he lives into eternity future, for he gives eternal life. What a grand, sweeping claim for the Son of God.

C. Suggested word studies

There are various words and phrases in this passage suggesting further study. Two of these are 'fellowship' and 'word of life.' Chapter 8 discusses the procedures of word study. Note that from the context of this paragraph it may be concluded that only eternally–living persons can have fellowship

- with one another,
- with the Father,
- and with the Son.

*   *   *

We have been probing the paragraph 1 John 1:1–4 to detect its message, especially as this is given by the group of its sentences, or verses. The next logical exercise is to study each particular verse in that paragraph. Verse study, therefore, is the subject of the next chapter.

Suggested Exercises

Analyze this key paragraph of Paul's epistles: Philippians 3:7–14. Using the King James Version, print the text phrase by phrase in a paragraph rectangle, (see page 82 for an example) showing relations and emphases. Observe how each verse is related to the previous one.

1. Who is the central person of the paragraph? What do we learn about him just in this paragraph?

2. Observe words that are repeated. Make a list of all the strong words of the paragraph.

3. Note how Paul intermingles testimony and aspiration.

4. Observe that all of verses 8–11 is one sentence. Show by diagram in the textual re–creation of your chart how each phrase is related to the surrounding ones. Observe especially the connecting word "that" (meaning "in order that").

5. Note the *positional* truth ("in him") in verse 9, and the *experiential* truth ("to know," "knowing") of the surrounding verses.

6. Study the time references: for example, the past (verses 7–8); present (verses 8–10); future (verses 11–14).

7. What is the core of the sentence of verses 13–14?

8. Compare "I count . . . loss" (verse 8) and "I count not" (verse 13).

9. Analyze carefully each small phrase of verse 10. Do the same for verse 14. How is verse 14 a climax of the paragraph?

10. Observe how Paul moves from the "I" of this paragraph to the "we" of the next.

7
Examining a Verse

In these chapters we have moved from the large to the small in the process of Bible study. We started with the whole Bible, and saw that though it is a library of sixty–six books, it is one book, with one main theme running throughout its many volumes.

When we surveyed one of the sixty–six books—Luke's Acts—we saw how important such a survey is as a preliminary step to analysis of individual chapters.

Next we learned how to study the Bible chapter by chapter, which is the heart of Bible analysis. Chapter study is perhaps the most common exercise in Bible study, because it is such a compact unit, and because it preserves and encourages context study. The example we used was from Joshua 5.

In the last chapter we focused on one paragraph—1 John 1:1–4—observing what it said, and how it said it.

Now, our attention is fixed on one verse. This "X–ray examination" penetrates to the underlying meaning beneath the surface of the text. The Bible is filled with these verses which are concentrates of larger truths. While most of these are not well known, there are many classic verses which have earned the reputation of being "golden texts" or "key verses." Many of these shine forth without being remembered for their surrounding context, like Hebrews 4:12. Others are stars in a galaxy of surrounding verses, like Romans 12:1. It is only known in heaven how many single Bible verses have been the basis for textual sermons.

We will examine just two verses as examples, noting the variety of truths revealed in such small compass. Of necessity the analysis made here can only be brief.

I. Examining Romans 1:16

> I am not ashamed of the gospel, because it is the power of God
> for the salvation of everyone who believes: first for the Jew,
> then for the Gentile.

A. Grammar

The core of the sentence is "I (subject) am not ashamed (verb) of the gospel (object)." This is a testimony, suggesting a courageous stand taken by one who might be tempted to be ashamed of the gospel—the temptation to hold back from preaching it at Rome (1:15) was real, or the testimony would not have been worded this way.

The strong verbs of the sentence are "ashamed" and "believes." The phrase "not ashamed" seems to suggest one aspect of what is involved in believing.

B. Type of content

There are various types of content in the Bible: history, doctrine, reflection (as in the Psalms), exhortation ("let us") and command, not to mention such special types as parables and apocalypse (Book of Revelation). This passage of Romans 1:16 is doctrinal, teaching truths about 1) the gospel of Christ, 2) the power of God, and 3) the salvation of sinners.

C. Facts

In chapter 5 we saw how Rudyard Kipling's "serving–men" (who, what, when, where, how, why), are helpful in Bible study. Miles Coverdale, in the preface to his 1535 English translation of the Bible, talked about these in the following famous lines:

> It shall greatly helpe ye to understande Scripture,
> If thou mark
> Not only what is spoken or wrytten,
> But of whom,
> And to whom,
> With what words,
> At what time,

Where,
To what intent,
With what circumstances,
Considering what goeth before
And what followeth.

1. *Application of the "serving men" to Romans 1:16:*

a) *who:* I (Paul), Christ, God, everyone, Jew, Greek.

b) *what:* gospel (Good News) is associated with Christ; power is associated with God; and salvation is associated with people (Jew and Gentile).

c) *when:* a continuing situation is implied by Paul's testimony of allegiance. Paul stood up for the gospel not only on occasion, but continually. Also, a word study on "believes," with the help of outside sources, would reveal that the believing is a continuous process.

There is another time reference in the verse. The phrase *"first* for the Jew" does not refer to priority of importance, but priority of time. In God's timetable of preaching of the gospel, the Jews heard it first, then the Gentiles.

d) *where:* the whole world of men. Everyone, everywhere.

e) *why* or *"what goeth before":* Paul was ready to preach the gospel at Rome (verse 15), because he was not ashamed of that gospel.

f) *how* or *"what followeth":* Verse 16 states that God can save sinners ("the power of God for . . . salvation"). Verse 17 tells what salvation really is: receiving the "righteousness from God." This is the answer to the fatal predicament of sin.

King James	Phillips	Living Testament	Today's English Version	New English Bible
"For I am not ashamed	"For I am not ashamed	"For I am not ashamed	"For I have complete confidence	"For I am not ashamed
of the gospel of Christ:	of the Gospel.	of this Good News about Christ.	in the gospel:	of the gospel.
for it is the power of God	I see it as the very power of God	It is God's powerful method	it is God's power	It is the saving
unto salvation	working for the salvation	of bringing to heaven	to save	power of God
to every one	of everyone	all	all	for everyone
that believeth;	who believes it;	who believe it.	who believe,	who has faith—
to the Jew first,	both Jew	This message was preached first to the Jews alone,	first the Jews	the Jew first,
and also to the Greek."	and Greek."	but now everyone is invited to come to God in this same way."	and also the Gentiles."	but the Greek also."

D. Shades of meaning

One of the most interesting experiences in Bible study is to compare various versions, to see the full spectrum of shades and colors in the words and phrases of a verse. The necessary economy of words in any one version limits how much the translator can write down as he translates. A comparison of versions, some of which are expanded paraphrases, can be helpful. (See adjacent chart.)

E. Outline the verse

All compound verses lend themselves to some outline. Romans 1:16 might look like this:

1. A Christian's stand for the gospel
2. God's power in the gospel
3. Universal audience of the gospel

Now try constructing your own outline.

F. Words to study

Strong words that invite further study are "ashamed," "gospel," "power," "salvation," and "believes." A word study of "power," for example, would reveal that the English word in this verse translates the Greek word *dunamos*, from which our word "dynamite" is derived.

*   *   *

Let us move on to another verse, following the same procedures as above.

II. Examining Hebrews 2:3

How shall we escape if we ignore such a great salvation? This salvation, which was first announced by the Lord, was confirmed to us by those who heard him.

(Note that a full analysis of verse 3 would include verses 2 and 4, which complete the thought of that sentence. Because of the limitation of space here, we will discuss only verse 3, but we will keep the context of the two surrounding verses in view. It will become plain, in fact, that verse 3 depends on verse 2 for its accurate interpretation.)

A. Grammar

This verse is obviously a rhetorical question, asked for effect, not for information. The expected response is, "We shall not, we cannot escape."

The core of the verse is, "We (subject) shall escape (verb) how (object)?"

The strong verbs of the verse are, "escape," "ignore," "announced," "confirmed," and "heard."

A textual re–creation of the verse reveals its interrelations, and shows the importance of the two small words "how" and "if." (See the chart below.)

"**HOW** shall we **ESCAPE**

    IF   we **IGNORE**   SUCH A GREAT SALVATION?

    . . . WHICH ⟵

    1) was first

    ANNOUNCED BY THE LORD,

    2) was **CONFIRMED** TO US

    BY THOSE WHO HEARD HIM."

B. Type of content
This verse is doctrinal and practical, with the impact of warning. The point is, we cannot escape recompense for neglecting so great a salvation as is ours, so let us see to it that we give earnest attention to it! If the "we" refers to Christians, as will be shown below, then this verse is practical teaching concerning Christian living.

C. Facts

1. *Application of the "serving men" to Hebrews* 2:3:

a) *who:* "we"; "the Lord"; "those who heard him." The "we" are believers, as indicated by the context. (Compare such verses as 1:2 ["us"]; 2:1,9; 3:1 ["we"].) This being the case, Hebrews 2:3 should be applied to Christians, and does not mean, at least in the intent of the setting, "How shall we escape [eternal judgment] if we [ignore] such a great salvation?"

b) *what:* There are two main subjects in this verse:
     1) the inescapable judgments, and
     2) ignoring the great salvation.

Every transgression brings recompense (2:2). This applies to everyone, including Christians. Unbelievers can *reject* what they do not have; Christians can *ignore* what they already have. (On the use of the word "ignore" or "neglect" recall Paul's words to Timothy: "Do not neglect your gift, which was given you" (1 Timothy 4:14). Hebrews tells of various ways we may neglect or ignore our salvation: by not obeying God's Word (2:1); not feeding on the solid food of the Word (5:11–6:20); not appropriating the privileges of prayer (10:19ff.); not believing (4:1–3). The unreasonableness and sinfulness of ignoring so great salvation is shown by reminding believers that the Lord himself—his message and his life—is being neglected.

c) ***when***: There is a time sequence in the verse:
1) the message of salvation is spoken by the Lord;
2) the message is confirmed by first–hand witnesses (and witnesses of signs, wonders, various miracles, gifts of the Holy Spirit—verse 4);
3) some may choose to ignore the message;
4) and for them there will be inevitable recompense. (No one can escape God's appointments of judgment!)

d) ***why***: Verse 2 says that in Old Testament days violation of God's Law ("the message spoken by angels") always brought recompense. This is a universal law of consequences, which applies to the words of the Lord (verse 3) in New Testament days as well. In fact there is an *a fortiori* argument here. In chapter 1 the writer of Hebrews shows Christ to be infinitely superior to the angels. The point now is, if the angels' words proved steadfast *how much more* (this is the *a fortiori* argument) the words of Christ.

e) ***how***: We have already seen that verse 4 is part of the sentence begun in verse 3. From 2:5 on, the writer magnifies Jesus the Son and Redeemer, and gives "a hundred and one" reasons and helps for the Christian *not* to ignore his great salvation.

D. Shades of Meaning

A translation comparison like we did for Romans 1:16 should be done for Hebrews 2:3.

—(The chart opposite compares five translations of Hebrews 2:3.)

King James	New International Version	Revised Standard Version	New American Standard	New English Bible
"How shall we escape,	"how shall we escape	"How shall we escape	"how shall we escape	"How, then, shall we escape
if we neglect	if we ignore	if we neglect	if we neglect	if we pay no attention to such
so great salvation; . . .	such a great salvation?	such a great salvation?	so great a salvation?	a great salvation?
began to be spoken by the Lord,	This salvation, which was first announced by the Lord,	It was declared at first by the Lord,	After it was at the first spoken through the Lord,	The Lord himself first announced this salvation,
and was confirmed unto us	was confirmed to us	and it was attested to us	it was confirmed to us	and those who heard him proved to us that it is true."
by them that heard him."	by those who heard him."	by those who heard him."	by those who heard."	

E. Outline the verse
1. The greatness of salvation
2. The Lord's proclamation of salvation
3. The truth of the message of salvation
4. The inescapable recompense for ignoring salvation

F. Words to study
The key word to study in this passage is "ignore." What does it mean to "ignore" one's salvation? Two other words for study: "escape," "salvation."

*   *   *

The study of single verses in the Bible is a very rewarding experience. It will usually lead you along other exciting paths of inquiry.

The variety of approaches in Bible study keeps you from falling into any routine of sameness, lameness, or tameness. Let it be part of your own study habits to analyze single verses in the Bible from time to time. Have fun with Bible study!

Below is a recommended list of verses for study. Some of these you may have already memorized, but have you ever analyzed them?

Sixty-six Golden Verses of the Bible[1]
Genesis 3:15—first Messianic promise
Exodus 12:13—life insurance
Leviticus 25:10—the Year of Jubilee
Numbers 9:17—the pilgrim's guide
Deuteronomy 29:29—the secret things
Joshua 1:8—the price of success
Judges 16:20—the lost power
Ruth 1:16—a shining example of constancy
1 Samuel 15:22—the indispensable virtue
2 Samuel 18:33—the father's lament
1 Kings 3:9—the prayer for wisdom
2 Kings 6:17—the divine reinforcements
1 Chronicles 4:10—a wonderful prayer in dark surroundings

2 Chronicles 16:9—the all–seeing eye
Ezra 7:10—the faithful scribe
Nehemiah 4:17—a true labor union
Esther 4:14—the woman for an emergency
Job 42:10—an enriching prayer
Psalm 84:11—the matchless Giver
Proverbs 3:15—the precious possession
Ecclesiastes 12:13—the great conclusion
Song of Songs 1:6—the unfaithful vineyard keeper
Isaiah 9:6—the most wonderful child
Jeremiah 29:13—the greatest discovery
Lamentations 3:22—God's unfailing mercies
Ezekiel 33:32—the sentimental hearers
Daniel 6:10—the unchangeable habit of prayer
Hosea 6:3—the road to divine blessing
Joel 2:28—the outpouring of the Spirit
Amos 8:11—the spiritual famine
Obadiah 4—the humbling of the proud
Jonah 1:3—an expensive journey
Micah 6:8—practical religion
Nahum 2:4—nothing new under the sun
Habakkuk 2:14—world–wide missions
Zephaniah 2:3—seeking the Lord
Haggai 2:4—a ringing call to duty
Zechariah 4:6—the true means of success
Malachi 3:10—the tither's promise
Matthew 7:7—the three–fold promise
Mark 16:15—the Great Commission
Luke 10:20—the real reason for joy
John 15:7—the master–key of prayer
Acts 1:8—the watchword of the spiritual campaign
Romans 10:9—the plan of salvation
1 Corinthians 3:11—the only foundation
2 Corinthians 4:6—the illuminated heart
Galatians 2:20—dying to live
Ephesians 4:13—the highest development
Philippians 2:5—the mind of Christ
Colossians 3:1—the heavenly ambition
1 Thessalonians 5:23—entire sanctification
2 Thessalonians 3:10—the duty to labor
1 Timothy 4:12—the young man's example

2 Timothy 2:4—the soldier's separation
Titus 2:14—the Redeemer's purpose
Philemon 15—a tender appeal
Hebrews 11:13—the pilgrims' vision
James 5:20—the soul-winner's achievement
1 Peter 1:18,19—the cost of redemption
2 Peter 1:21—the origin of prophecy
1 John 3:2—the sons of God
2 John 6—love and obedience
3 John 4—the minister's joy
Jude 24, 25—the divine keeper
Revelation 11:15—the consummation of the divine plan

Suggested Exercises

The most widely memorized verse in the Bible is perhaps John 3:16. Because of its familiarity it is often overlooked for close scrutiny and analysis. See what you can do with a thorough analysis of this great verse.

1. Examine the verse's neighbors—that is, verses 14–15 and 17. Keep this context in mind.
2. Analyze the grammar of the verse. For example, what is the core?
3. Look for the who, what, where, when, how and why.
4. What would you choose to be the key word or phrase of the verse?
5. Compare the beginning and end of the verse.
6. Are there any contrasts in the verse?
7. What do you see here of cause and effect?
8. What words are picture words? What words are theological?
9. Construct an outline for the verse.
10. What truths, if any, are implied?
11. What words of this verse call for special word study?
12. Compare the reading of the verse in a few modern versions.

8
Weighing a Word

The study of a single Bible word—carefully weighing its content and function—can be one of the most fascinating exercises of your study. Wilbur M. Smith writes, "There is no book in the world whose words will yield such treasures of truth, such spiritual richness, such rivers of refreshing water, such strengthening of the soul as the words with which the Holy Spirit has inspired the authors of the books of our Bible."[1]

I. God's Inspired Words

When we consider how many different words there are in the Bible, we might wonder what weight one word can have among so many.[2] The challenge to read such a large book may seem impossible to fulfill, but it should encourage us to realize that Bible reading and study are designed to *last a lifetime*.[3] Just as a great door swings on small hinges, the important theological statements of the Bible often depend upon even the smallest words, such as prepositions and articles. Using a further analogy, one writer has said that, as the smallest dewdrop on the meadow at night has a star sleeping in its bosom, so the most insignificant passage of Scripture has in it a shining truth.

Hebrew and Greek scholars invite us to see the rich language found in these ancient testaments. Robert B. Girdlestone says this about the Hebrew language:

Its definite article . . . its mode of marking emphasis and comparison, the gravity and solemnity of its structure, the massive dignity of its style, the picturesqueness of its idiom—these make it peculiarly fitting for the expression of sacred truth.[4]

Richard C. Trench speaks as enthusiastically for the Greek language:

[The Greek language was] spoken by a people of the subtlest intellect; who saw distinctions, where others saw none; who divided out to different words what others often were content to huddle confusedly under a common term; who were themselves singularly alive to its value, diligently cultivating the art of synonymous distinction . . .; and who have bequeathed a multitude of fine and delicate observations on the right discrimination of their own words to the afterworld.[5]

But how does this pertain to those of us who are not acquainted with the Hebrew or Greek, and who might very well say, "It's *all* Greek to me"? Can the beauty, depth, and fullness buried in the original manuscripts be converted to English? This subtlety of interpretation has always been a great challenge to Bible translators. In chapter 1 of this book we showed that the Bible is a miraculous book in that God *inspired* gifted people to record his laws and thoughts. Similarly, the King James translators, relying heavily upon the earlier work of William Tyndale and John Wycliffe, were supremely gifted in matching the excellence of the Hebrew and Greek versions:

But always in considering this, our English classic [King James Version], we must remember that behind it were the world's profoundest religious truths uttered by Hebrews in concrete, vivid, figurative expression. It was this rich ore which was cast into the English crucible to be heated hot with religious fervor and with the zest of a new intellectual awakening. . . . Out of the fire came this book, so simple, direct, and suggestive in language, so beautiful and resonant in rhythm, so majestic and inspiring in tone that as literature it is said even to surpass the original, and no one influence has been so

great in the life of English–speaking people, religiously, mor-
ally, socially, politically, as has this version.[6]

It is encouraging to know that the words which God
inspired in the original languages have not been watered
down, over the centuries, in the translation process.

The only place where God has chosen to record the full
revelation of eternal life is in the Bible—a book wrapped in
the "swaddling–clothes" of human words. Surely, if we
are to know the *Word*, we must study the *words*. There
are two basic ways to learn the full meaning of a Bible
word: the context approach and the comparative approach.

A. Context approach

Here we study a word to learn its contribution and
function in the context of an isolated verse, paragraph, or
chapter. Examples of this approach were given in the earlier chapters. For the context approach study, let's suppose we are studying the word "faith" as it appears ten
times in the fourth chapter of Romans. Some questions
we might ask are:

1. What would we know about faith if this chapter
   were the entire Scripture?
2. Could any other word have served the same purposes in these ten references?
3. How much does the chapter contribute to the
   meaning of the word faith; and how much does the
   word faith contribute to the meaning of the chapter? Although a concordance reveals that the *word*
   faith appears ten times in the chapter, it is clear
   that the *concept* of faith is described and illustrated in various ways. For example, look at
   Abraham's faith, and see the various shades and
   qualities of that faith as they are progressively recorded in verses 17–21:

   • He considered *hopeful* what appeared *hope-
     less*: "Against all hope, Abraham in hope be-
     lieved" (v. 18).

- He accepted as *possible* what appeared *impossible*: "Without weakening in his faith, he faced the fact that his body was as good as dead" (v. 19).
- He didn't doubt the great promise of God: "he did not waver through unbelief regarding the promise of God" (v. 20).
- He placed full assurance in the omnipotence of God: "being fully persuaded that God had power to do what he had promised" (v. 21).

Each of the above four references presents a different *shade* of what real faith is.

B. Comparative approach

This method of studying a word, a restricted form of topical study, observes how a particular word is used throughout the entire Bible. The remainder of this chapter is about this comparative method.

There are three main rules for weighing a Bible word, to learn its total contribution to the Scriptures. Let's apply them to the Bible word "fullness."

1. *Check its occurrences in the Bible.* For this, we need the help of an exhaustive concordance. Strong's *Exhaustive Concordance* and Young's *Analytical Concordance*[7] are the standard works. References below are to the former.

Some strong words of the Bible appear so often that it may not be possible, in a study exercise limited by time, to refer to every verse cited by the concordance (i.e., the word "heaven"). In such cases, by reading the *verse excerpts* that surround each listing for the word in the concordance we are usually able to select those verses most applicable to our study. The word "fullness" does not appear that often, and so we are easily able to read all the references. When we first locate the word "fullness" in the concordance, we see:

- number of occurrences: twenty–five

- distribution as to testament: about equally divided
- books where the word appears more frequently: Psalms (six times) and Ephesians (four times)
- pattern of appearance: It is interesting to note that, except for the one reference in John, Paul is the only New Testament writer to use the word.

2. *Find the root meaning.* Now we get to the heart of our study, which is, what does the word mean? An English dictionary will help define the English word, but why not search for the word's meaning in the original languages, if this is possible? The directions below show how you can make a non–technical study of the root meanings of the Hebrew and Greek words.

There are various outside helps for this kind of study.[8] You can learn much, however, from Strong's *Exhaustive Concordance,* which gives a number opposite each reference—each number representing the Hebrew or Greek word which the English word translates. The Old Testament references of course refer to Hebrew words (listed by number in the back of the concordance under "Hebrew and Chaldee Dictionary"); the New Testament references refer to Greek words (listed by number under "Greek Dictionary of the New Testament"). Similar numbers (e.g., 4393 and 4395) usually refer to the same roots.

OT references for "fullness"
Group One:

> 4395—Numbers 18:27
>
> 4393—Deuteronomy 33:16; 1 Chronicles 16:32; Psalms 24:1; 50:12; 89:11; 96:11; 98:7; Ezekiel 19:7
>
> 4390—Job 20:22

Group Two:
>   7648—Psalm 16:11
>   7653—Ezekiel 16:49

NT references for "fullness"
>   4138—All the NT references use one Greek
>   word—John 1:16; Romans 11:12,25; 15:29; 1
>   Corinthians 10:26,28; Galatians 4:4; Ephesians
>   1:10,23; 3:19; 4:13; Colossians 1:19; 2:9

When we consult the Hebrew and Greek dictionaries at the back of the concordance, we find:

Hebrew
>   4390—The root is *mawlaw,* meaning "to fill or be
>   full of." We read Job 20:22, KJV, in the light of
>   this: "In the fulness (KJV spelling) of his suffi-
>   ciency he shall be in straits."
>   4393—*Melo,* from 4390. "All that is therein."
>   When we read the verses using this form of
>   the word, we find they are all similar. For
>   example: "The earth is the Lord's, and the
>   *fulness* thereof . . ." (Psalm 24:1, KJV).
>   4395—Traced back to the root of 4390, *mawlaw.*
>   "Something fulfilled," that is, "abundance of pro-
>   duce." The one verse using this form is Num-
>   bers 18:27, KJV, with its reference to "the *ful-
>   ness* of the winepress."

Now we turn to the second group of numbers—7648 and 7653, which suggests a different root from the one we have been using:
>   7648—The concordance directs us to the num-
>   ber 7646, which shows the root *sawbah,* mean-
>   ing "to fill to satisfaction." The key word here is
>   *satisfaction.*
>   7653—The same root, *sawbah.* Here we see
>   verses using this *different* word "fulness":

>> Thou wilt show me the path of life: in thy pres-
>> ence *is fulness* of joy; at thy right hand *there
>> are* pleasures for evermore.
>>   (Psalm 16:11, KJV, italics added).

> Behold, this was the iniquity of thy sister
> Sodom, pride, *fulness* of bread, and abundance
> of idleness was in her . . .
> > (Ezekiel 16:49, KJV, italics added).

Our tentative conclusion is that the "fulness" of this second group (*sawbah*) has a different connotation from the "fulness" of the first group (*mawlaw*). *Mawlaw* connotes full scope; *sawbah* connotes full satisfaction.

Now we turn to the New Testament references:

Greek

> 4138. The word is *pleroma*, traced back to the root *pimplemi* (4130): "fill, fulfill, accomplish, furnish."

The observation we make here is that this Greek root has the same connotation as the Hebrew *mawlaw* (fullness as to scope), not the root *sawbah* (fullness as to satisfaction).

With the above root meanings in mind, we read the various New Testament verses, where the Old Testament picture of *mawlaw*, a full unit—with no voids—is applied to theological truths, (e.g., "and of his *fullness* have all we received, and grace for grace"). All of the verses seem to use the word "fullness" in the same way, with the possible exception of Romans 15:29, where the idea of satisfaction *appears* to be meant, because of the word "blessing" in the context. A further study will clarify this.

3. *Recognize its usage.* The *root meaning* of a word sheds light on the word's origin, but in the final analysis the *usage* of the word is the primary determinant of its meaning.

a) *Usage in extra–biblical literature.* Except for an exhaustive study of the word by the advanced student, this step of investigation is not necessary. For those interested in pursuing it, special works would have to be consulted.[9] Here we learn, for example, how people on the street used the Greek word *pimplemi* outside of any religious context. A fourth century manuscript has this phrase: "Fill (*pimplemi*) the vessel with green mustard."[10] This shows that the New Testament writers used the word in the same way the word was used in everyday life. We are told that the word *pleroma* probably was not used often in the vernacular. One manuscript, dated 240 B.C., writes, "You wrote me not to withdraw the gang (*pleroma*) from Philoteris before they had finished the work." The word here means "full company" or "complement."

b) *Usage in the Bible.* How a word is used in the Bible indicates the precise meaning of that word.

- *first usage in the Bible:* It is always interesting to see how certain words were used in their first biblical appearance. For example, note how the word "knowledge" was used in Genesis 2:9. We must be careful, however, not to suppose that the first usage of a word in the Bible must determine the meaning of the word in all subsequent appearances.

- *most frequent usage in the Bible:* We have seen that the word "fullness" is used in two different ways in the Bible: 1) full scope and, 2) total satisfaction. The former is the most common; the latter appears only in two of the twenty–five occurrences.

- *comparison of Old and New Testament usages:* Old Testament — word is used both ways. New Testament — word is used only with the meaning of full scope.

- *areas of application:* Look briefly at the word "fullness" as it appears in its most common form — that of full scope (Hebrew *mawlaw* and Greek *pleroma*). Here we want to note the various areas of its application. By comparing and collating the verses, the following outline emerges:

I. The Material World

  A. Fullness of nature

    1. *Earth* (Deuteronomy 33:16; Psalm 24:1; 1 Corinthians 10:26,28)

    2. *Land* (Ezekiel 19:7)

    3. *World* (Psalm 50:12; 89:11)

    4. *Sea* (1 Chronicles 16:32; Psalm 96:11; 98:7)

    5. *Winepress* (Numbers 18:27)

B. Fullness of things

    1. *Possessions* (Job 20:22). The interesting lesson to learn here is that wealth does not help the real plight of the wicked man: "he shall be in straits."

II. The Spiritual World

A. Fullness of the Trinity

    1. *God* (Ephesians 3:19)

    2. *Godhead* (Colossians 1:19; 2:9)

    3. *Christ* (John 1:16; Ephesians 4:13)

B. Fullness of the message of God

    1. *The Gospel's blessing* (Romans 15:29)

C. Fullness of the family of God

    1. *Israel* (Romans 11:12)

    2. *Church* (Ephesians 1:23)

D. Fullness of the calendar of God

    1. *Time* (Galatians 4:4)

    2. *Times* (Ephesians 1:10)

    3. *Gentiles* (Romans 11:25)

The above outline should suggest many blessed truths. For example, the fullness of the blessing of Christ's gospel (Romans 15:29) is for us today. How big is it? Can we even measure it? We may not comprehend such total blessing, but taking the phrase "*fulness* of the earth" (Psalm 24:1, KJV) as a quantitative measuring stick, we are overwhelmed by Paul's reference to the immensity of the gospel's blessing.

Consider "the *fulness* of God" (Ephesians 3:19, KJV). We can easily accept such a theological phrase, for God is the Cause of all things, creating and upholding his universe. But it is difficult to believe that we can be filled with God. And yet Paul was inspired of the Spirit to record this very practical, glorious truth, that you can be "filled with all the *fulness* of God."

Do we have goals for our Christian journey? Have we ever considered the goal of the "*fulness* of Christ" (Ephesians 4:13)? That was the goal Paul was interested in: "Till we all come in the unity of the faith, . . . unto the measure of the stature of the fulness of Christ." There surely is no higher goal in life.

These kinds of thoughts come to you when you study the Word. God invites us into this full understanding and appreciation of himself in this way.

Key Bible Words for Comparative Study

access	holy	reconcile
atone	Immanuel	redeem
baptize	iniquity	repent
believe	Jehovah	rest
bless	Jesus	righteous
chasten	kingdom	sabbath
Christ	know	sacrifice
church	law	saint
covenant	life	save
death	Lord	sin
disciple	love	spirit
evil	manifest	temptation
faint	mercy	truth
favor	minister	understand

fellowship	name	vain
good	obey	vision
gospel	passover	watch
grace	peace	wisdom
hear	perfect	word
hell	preach	

Suggested Exercises

1. A key word in the Bible is "love." A concordance will reveal how often it appears in both testaments.

2. Make a study of the word as it appears in the New Testament. Observe from the concordance that there are two main New Testament words for love: one which translates *agapao* (number 25 in Strong's concordance); and one which translates *phileo* (number 5368).

3. Study John 21:15–17 for an interesting juxtaposition of the two Greek words. Continue your comparative study by observing how the words are used in other verses, separately.

4. Concentrate your study on the word which translates *agapao*. Arrive at a full definition of the word. (Note: a topical study of "love" will be made at the end of chapter 9.)

9
Organizing a Topic

Topical Bible study is a "customized" type of study, usually arising out of a particular situation or need. For instance, as we read about the Arab–Israeli conflict in the newspapers, we may like to know what the Bible says about the Jewish people. And so we make a topical study of this subject. Ecumenical stirrings suggest a study of church history; the charismatic movement, a study about gifts of the Spirit; and battles between nations, a study about war. Topical sermons delivered from the pulpits are based on just such topical studies.

Topical study goes one step further than word study. While word study stays within the boundaries of analyzing the meaning of the particular word itself, topical study moves freely about a general subject, studying synonyms, antonyms, and even references that are only implied in passages. A concordance is of limited help to us here.

However, there are other outside helps that are useful for topical study. *The Zondervan Topical Bible*[1] was compiled particularly to serve this kind of study. For the study of doctrines, books on theology are very helpful.

I. Procedure of Topical Study

The procedure is simple, following a natural inductive approach. With this process, you begin with unrelated facts and then bring them together into an organized whole. The procedure is described as follows:

A. Build a list of Bible references

At this point we are not so concerned with reading the passages themselves, as we are in finding the references. To find these, we start with a concordance, then move on to other source books, such as that mentioned above. The references are listed in one column, on the left–hand side of the paper, leaving room for later notations.

Suppose we wanted to study the subject of *angels*, with special reference to good angels. Some of the verses which we would come up with, from the above sources, would be:

Genesis 3:24; 6:2,4; 19:11–13
Deuteronomy 18:10–12
1 Samuel 4:4
2 Samuel 14:20
2 Kings 19:15
Nehemiah 9:6
Job 1:6; 2:1; 33:23; 38:4–7
Psalm 18:9–10; 68:17; 80:1; 91:11; 99:1; 103:20; 104:4; 148:2,5
Isaiah 6:1–2, 6; 8:19–20
Ezekiel 9:1,5,7; 10:1–20; 28:14–16
Daniel 3:28; 6:22; 7:10, 16; 9:21; 10:13, 21; 12:1
Matthew 1:20; 4:11; 13:39, 49–50; 16:27; 18:10; 22:30; 24:36; 26:53; 28:2–7
Luke 1:26–38; 2:8–15; 4:34; 16:22; 20:34–36; 22:43
John 1:51
Acts 1:11; 5:19; 12:7, 11, 23
1 Corinthians 6:3; 10:20–21
Ephesians 1:21; 6:12
Colossians 1:16; 2:18
1 Thessalonians 4:16–18
2 Thessalonians 1:7
1 Timothy 4:1; 5:21; 6:16
Hebrews 1:6–7, 14; 2:16; 12:22–23; 13:2
1 Peter 1:12
2 Peter 2:11
Jude 9
Revelation 5:11; 9:20–21; 12:7–12; 14:6; 21:1–2,12

B. Read the various passages

As we read, we jot down on paper opposite each reference the main truths taught about angels by each verse. Brief notations are recommended, to help in our next step of organization.

C. Organize individual facts under topical headings

To do this, we first read over the brief notations we have recorded for each verse, correlating passages of similar teaching. Eventually, in this step of synthesizing, each verse will fall under one group of common content. Then the groups will suggest an outline. For the subject of angels, it might look like this:

I.   Origin of Angels

   A. Creation

   B. Time of their creation

   C. Number

II. Nature of Angels

   A. Not glorified human beings

   B. Incorporeal (having no body)

   C. A company; not a race

   D. Powers

III. Ministry of Good Angels

   A. Past ministry

   B. Present ministry

   C. Future ministry

II. Two Kinds of Topical Study

There are two different kinds of topical study: broad, and explicit. Listed below are samples of each:

A. Broad subjects
1. Characters of the Bible (e.g., patriarchs, martyrs, kings, women, disciples)
2. Crises of the Bible
3. Key doctrines of the Bible
4. Prayers of the Bible
5. Conversions of the Bible
6. Sermons of the Bible
7. Calls to service

B. Explicit subjects
1. Names of God
2. Titles of Jesus
3. Crises of Jesus' life
4. Parables of Jesus
5. Invitations of Jesus
6. Ten great sermons of Acts (five by Peter; one by Stephen; four by Paul)
7. Paul the missionary
8. The six "precious" things of Peter's epistles
9. The seven "blesseds" and eight "overcomeths" of Revelation
10. The "better" things of Hebrews
11. The "I am's" of John
12. The "fear of the Lord" of Proverbs
13. The seven "forty days" of the Bible

Perhaps the most interesting and enlightening kind of topical study is the study of a Bible character. We are mainly *onlookers* when we read about historical events; we are intimate *participators* when we read biography or phy. Studying the life experiences of people of fords a vicarious experience of the Lord for us Sometimes, we can intimately relate to their , when we recall how the Lord similarly

Almost three–thousand men and women appear by name in the text of the Bible. A large amount of biographical data is given for many of these. A Bible dictionary usually supplies the main biblical references pertaining to any one Bible character. Whenever we study the life of a person in the Bible, we should look for the following:

1. Name(s); surname; and significance of each
2. Ancestry—what does the Bible say of the parents?
3. Environment; training
4. Desirable and undesirable traits
5. Friendships
6. Conversion; other crises
7. Influence by others and upon others
8. Spiritual growth
9. Work accomplished
10. Sins and shortcomings
11. Years lived

* * *

There is hardly a subject of human interest that is *not* treated in the Bible. Even such modern areas as space, psychology, teaching methods, riots, authority, law, and taxes appear throughout. Bible encyclopedias and dictionaries attest to the vast scope of material found in the Bible. This is noteworthy in view of the fact that it does not pretend to be a textbook in such areas as the arts and sciences. John Greenleaf Whittier expresses it this way:

> We search the world for truth. We cull
> The good, the pure, the beautiful
> From graven stone and written scroll,
> And all old flower–fields of the soul;
> And, weary seekers of the best,
> We come back laden from our quest,
> To find that all the sages said
> Is in the Book our mothers read.

Nothing recorded in the Bible is superfluous. Everything contributes in some way to the grand theme of

God's Offer of Salvation to Mankind by Jesus Christ. The many kinds of extensive topical studies that may be derived from the Scriptures suggest how vast and all–inclusive the theme actually is.

Suggested Exercises

1. Barnabas is an interesting New Testament character, from whose life some important spiritual lessons may be learned. Study every New Testament verse with reference to him, and make a list of the practical lessons being taught.

2. Continue the study of the word "love" begun in the previous chapter. Observe the various aspects of agape in the New Testament, and arrive at an outline of the topic. Such an outline might include a) divine love, b) walk of Christian love, c) fruits of love. Choose from a concordance the verses you want to use in your study. For a shorter study of the word, identify what each of the following verses teaches about love:

   Matthew 5:43-48; 22:37-40
   John 3:16; 13:35; 16:27; 17:23-24
   Romans 5:5, 8; 8:31-39; 12:9; 13:8-10
   1 Corinthians 13:4-7, 13; 16:22
   2 Corinthians 5:14-15
   Galatians 2:20; 5:13
   Ephesians 2:4-5
   Colossians 3:14
   1 Thessalonians 4:9
   Titus 2:4
   Hebrews 12:6-11
   1 John 3:18; 4:8-10, 16

PART III
Applying the Bible

10
Putting the Bible to Work

Hopefully, this book has helped you to gain a greater appreciation of the Bible, along with suggesting ways to approach Scripture study and analysis. But, ultimately, the goal in Scripture study is not to do something to the Bible, but to let it do something to us. When a young Chinese student was asked how he was getting along in his Bible study, he replied, "I am now reading the Bible and behaving it." The following simple diagrams serve to illustrate the importance of application in Bible study.

This circle represents the Bible, which is the Word of God:

What a mighty Word it is! Its potential is beyond all comprehension. Its message—the gospel—is dynamic (Romans 1:16). God wants this Word to be at the center of our lives—instructing, motivating, and empowering us. Put this circle in the center of a larger circle, which represents our lives:

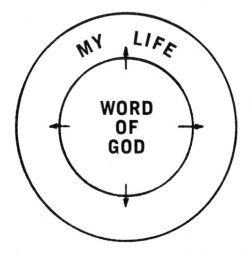

The arrows represent the ever–active work of the Word. In its work of diagnosis, the Word exposes the cancer of sin and brings conviction (Hebrews 4:12–13). In its healing work it cleans and purifies (John 15:3; 17:17; Ephesians 5:25–26). Its manna gives strength for living (Deuteronomy 8:3), and its sword equips us for battle (Ephesians 6:17). As a manual it guides us along the right paths (Psalm 119:24), and as waters flowing from the throne of God it brings forth fruit to the glory of God (Psalm 1:2–3). There is no book in all the world like this! The writer Izaak Walton (1593–1683) penned four short lines to tell what the Bible meant in his life:

Every hour I read you,
  kills a sin,
Or lets a virtue in
  to fight against it.

But there is a larger ministry of the Word. This ministry, launched in the Great Commission (Matthew 28:19–20), affects the whole world. So put the circle of the Word, and of My Life, in the center of the circle of The World:

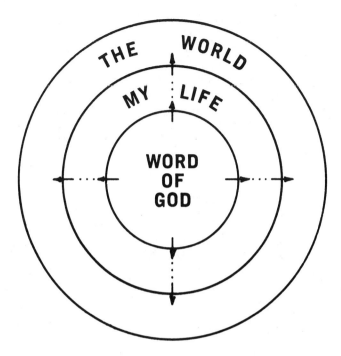

Again, the arrows represent the activity of the Word—the Word not just working *in* my life—but, also, working *through* my life in the world. This is God's full design for putting the Bible to work.

Both the Old and New Testaments have two basic thrusts: to point unbelievers *to* God, and to show believers how to walk *with* God. Paul made this clear when he wrote his last inspired letter to Timothy, reminding his friend and co–laborer that the holy Scriptures which Timothy had learned from childhood (at that time the Scriptures included only the Old Testament) were able to make him "wise for salvation" (2 Timothy 3:15). This was teaching concerning the *way to God*. Also, Paul wrote, all Scripture was given by God "so that the man of God may be thoroughly equipped for every good work" (2 Timothy 3:17). Paul was telling Timothy that the Scriptures were to equip him to walk acceptably with his God. This was teaching concerning our *walk with God*. All spiritual lessons from passages of the Bible have something to say, directly or indirectly, about the *way* to God, or the *walk* with God.

When we are convinced that the Bible offers up–to–date instruction, that it concerns us personally, and that its spiritual lessons are not hazy or ambiguous, we are more likely to apply its counsel. This suggests some important rules for applying Scriptures to everyday life:

I. Expect the Bible to Teach Vital Truths

There is a rule that the Bible student who expects much from the Bible will see much; and one who dabbles in it will find no more than a smattering of wisdom. The Bible is unique because it teaches *crucial* doctrines (cf. 2 Timothy 3:16). The most important of these concern:

A. Who God is

B. Who man is

C. What God does for man

What subjects are more vital and contemporary than these? Whenever you study a passage in the Bible, notice what it says about God (Father, Son, Holy Spirit), or about man, or about God's ways with man, and make some personal applications based on your observations. For example, What do you see in the following verses: "In that day the Lord Almighty will be a glorious crown, a beautiful wreath for the remnant of his people" (Isaiah 28:5); and "God's judgment against those who do such things is based on truth" (Romans 2:2). How would you apply this to your life?

The Bible reproves, convicts, corrects, instructs, inspires, challenges, and motivates. What can be more inspiring than Psalm 23; more challenging than Joshua 24:15; more motivational than 1 Corinthians 15:58!

II. The Bible Involves You Personally

If you think you are living in semi–privacy or isolation, think again. Inescapably, you are related in some way to God, to Satan, and to other people, as well as to yourself. Here is a more detailed look at those relationships:

A. Your relationship with God

- fellowship to enjoy
- commands to obey
- promises to claim
- prayers to echo

B. Your relationship to Satan

- person to resist
- devices to recognize
- sins to avoid
- armor to wear

C. You and others

- in the home
- in the church
- in society
- in the world

D. Yourself

- past heritage
- present experience
- future hope

Try reading through a chapter in the Bible, making a note of everything it says about some of the items listed above. Two suggested chapters are Psalm 144 and John 11.

III. Life Application

It is not difficult to know how to apply a simple command like "Do everything without complaining or arguing" (Philippians 2:14), but can spiritual lessons be derived from other types of passages? Consider:

> So David gave orders to assemble the aliens living in Israel, and from among them he appointed stonecutters to prepare dressed stone for building the house of God (1 Chronicles 22:2).

How do you apply *that* passage to your life?

A. Context and content
Locate the passage in the general scheme of the Bible. There are four categories:

1. *Teaching and Laws* (Genesis–Deuteronomy)
2. *History* (Genesis–Esther)
3. *Reflection* (Job–Song of Songs)
4. *Prophecy* (Isaiah–Malachi)

After you locate the category under which your passage falls, determine the type of writing. This is better explained by consulting the diagram opposite.

A diagram such as this offers a category for every passage in the Bible. When you label a passage in this way, you are helping yourself to think clearly and categorically about the Bible and its life applications. Notice that Christ is at the center. Many Old Testament passages are messianic, foretelling Christ. All New Testament passages following the Gospels are based on the life, death and resurrection of Christ.

B. Old Testament applications
Is the passage one of *laws*? First determine how this might relate to Christ—then involve yourself. For example, the burnt offering of Leviticus 1:3 is a "male without defect"; the offerer "shall offer it of his own voluntary will" (1:3, KJV). In its present day application, Christ is the

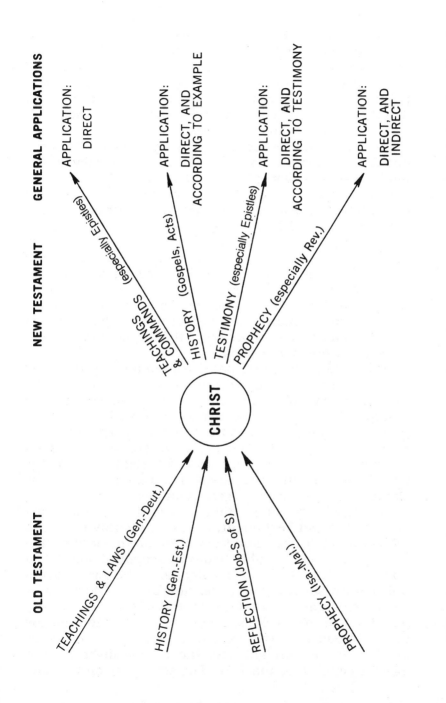

OLD TESTAMENT

TEACHINGS & LAWS (Gen.-Deut.)

HISTORY (Gen.-Est.)

REFLECTION (Job-S of S)

PROPHECY (Isa.-Mal.)

CHRIST

NEW TESTAMENT

TEACHINGS & COMMANDS (especially Epistles)

HISTORY (Gospels, Acts)

TESTIMONY (especially Epistles)

PROPHECY (especially Rev.)

GENERAL APPLICATIONS

APPLICATION: DIRECT

APPLICATION: DIRECT, AND ACCORDING TO EXAMPLE

APPLICATION: DIRECT, AND ACCORDING TO TESTIMONY

APPLICATION: DIRECT, AND INDIRECT

sacrifice "without defect," and the Christian, in an act of consecration, identifies himself with Christ "of his own voluntary will."

Is the passage one of *history*? Again, the events might point forward to Christ, such as the Exodus from Egypt being a type of the redemption of a sinner from the bondage of Satan. In any event, the *example* of how to approach God and live acceptably to him appears throughout Old Testament history. Abraham's journey to the land of Canaan (Genesis 12:1–4) shows faith and obedience in action. Paul states: "These things happened . . . as examples and were written down as warnings for us" (1 Corinthians 10:11).

Is the passage one of *testimony, prayer,* or *reflection,* such as is found in the poetic and wisdom literature? If so, there is little difficulty in making life applications, for the experiences of people are universal experiences—we were all created alike, and we are all sinners in need of the same Savior. Psalm 51, the great penitential prayer of David, is an example of Scripture that is personally applicable every day of our lives.

Prophetical Scripture passages remind you that God is an omniscient Designer and sovereign Master of history. They can stir your heart to an increased devotion and faith in your God and Savior. If it is Old Testament prophecy fulfilled (such as the death of Christ foretold in Isaiah 53), apply it to your life in view of the event's accomplishment. If the prophecy is futuristic (such as the Lord's coming and the Great Tribulation foretold by Daniel), respond to the urgent reminder.

The key to applying a Bible passage to your life, especially in the Old Testament, is first to identify the local, temporal detail, then find the universal, timeless principle. "Remember the Sabbath day by keeping it holy" (Exodus 20:8). Here the Jewish calendar is the temporal detail; a universal principle, applicable to both Old and New Testament times, is that we should observe one designated day of the week especially as a holy day unto the Lord. Consider another example. "Achan . . . took some of [the devoted things]. So the Lord's anger burned against Israel" (Joshua 7:1). The story goes on to relate that Israel lost heart and thirty–six men were slain—all because of one man's sin. Such was the local event of that moment. Here we discover a timeless principle—that sin in one man has the potential to adversely affect the whole group.

C. New Testament applications

The New Testament is usually easier to apply than the Old Testament, mainly because we are living in the same age as its writers and original readers. The applications themselves are generally the same as for the Old Testament, because the same *kinds* of writings comprise the New Testament:

1. *Teachings and commands*—found especially in the Epistles. Applications are usually direct, clear, and timeless. For example, "Let us love one another" (1 John 4:7).
2. *History*—mainly the Gospels and Acts. Sins to avoid and examples to follow abound here.
3. *Testimony*—found especially in the Epistles. True Christians join in heart with the New Testament writers whenever a testimony is read, such as Paul's "I know whom I have believed, and am convinced that he is able to guard what I have entrusted to him for that day" (2 Timothy 1:12).
4. *Prophecy*—found throughout the New Testament, but especially in Revelation. Studying prophecy increases one's faith, inspires service in taking the gospel to lost souls, and is an incentive to righteous living. Peter said, "Since everything will be destroyed in this way, what kind of people ought you to be? You ought to live holy and godly lives as you look forward to the day of God and speed its coming" (2 Peter 3:11–12).

*   *   *

In applying the Bible to everyday life, it is not enough to know what the Bible *says*. Paul in his letter to Titus spoke of the need of *adorning* the doctrine of God (Titus

2:10, KJV), and throughout the letter he showed that good *deeds* were that adorning (i.e. 2:14). While James' emphasis was, "Faith without works is dead" (James 2:20, KJV), Paul's emphasis was, "Doctrine without deeds is bare." If we truly enjoy reading and studying the Bible, we will enjoy putting it into practice. The psalmist was so thrilled about the Scriptures that he exclaimed:

> Oh, how I love your law!
> I meditate on it all day long. (119:97).

Seven lines later he supported this testimony with a word about deeds:

> I have kept my feet from every evil path
> so that I might obey your word (119:101).

May such total *enjoyment* of God's Word be our daily portion!

Appendix

READING THROUGH THE BIBLE IN 3 YEARS

	FIRST YEAR	SECOND YEAR	THIRD YEAR
JAN.	MARK	PSALMS 42-72	1 and 2 KINGS
FEB.	GENESIS	ROMANS & HEBREWS	PSALMS 107-150
MAR.		ECCLESIASTES	
		NUMBERS	JEREMIAH - LAMENTATIONS
APR.	ACTS	JOB	EZRA - NEHEMIAH - ESTHER
			SONG of SONGS
MAY	EXODUS	GALATIANS to COLOSSIANS	1 and 2 CHRONICLES
JUNE		DEUTERONOMY	HOSEA to MALACHI
JUL.	PSALMS 1-41	1 PETER to 3 JOHN	JAMES, JUDE, PHILEMON
AUG.	MATTHEW	PSALMS 73-106	ISAIAH
SEP.	LEVITICUS	JOHN	
OCT.	PROVERBS	JOSHUA	1 TIM. - TITUS - 2 TIM.
		JUDGES - RUTH	
NOV.	EZEKIEL-DANIEL	CORINTHIANS-THESSALONIANS	LUKE
DEC.	REVELATION	1 and 2 SAMUEL	

The above sequence has been arranged with topical order and variety in mind. As you begin each new book, determine the length of each daily reading, according to the time-span allotted.

Notes

Chapter 3

1. Richard G. Moulton, *A Short Introduction to the Literature of the Bible* (Boston: D. C. Heath and Co., 1901), iii–iv, emphasis added.

2. *The Everyday Bible* (Fort Worth, Texas: Worthy Publishing, 1987) and the paperback *Everyday New Testament* (Minneapolis: World Wide Publications, 1988) are recent examples of this. Initially planned for age–groups through grade four, this version has become popular with all groups and ages, including home-makers, college students, and professional people.

3. The World Wide Publications edition of *The Everyday New Testament* includes background notes on each NT book, along with Bible–study methods and full-page notes on key NT subjects.

4. William Law, *A Serious Call to the Devout and Holy Life* (London: Aldine House, 1898), 219.

5. Clyde Tombaugh, *Time* (April 1, 1966), 10.

6. Irving Jensen, *Independent Bible Study* (Chicago: Moody Press, 1963).

7. Wilbur M. Smith, *Profitable Bible Study* (Boston: W. A. Wilde Company, 1939), 65–67.

8. *The NIV Study Bible* (Grand Rapids, Michigan: Zondervan Publishing House, 1985), explains difficult passages.

Chapter 4

1. Your chapter titles should be vivid single words or short phrases taken directly from the text which serve as clues to the content of the chapter. They are not intended to make a formal outline of the book as such.

2. For example, James Strong, *The Exhaustive Concordance of the Bible* (New York: Abingdon Press, 1890).

3. If you are interested in a Bible–study manual which will help you continue your analytical studies in Acts, you may want to refer to this author's *Acts (Do It Yourself Bible Study Series),* (San Bernardino, California: Here's Life Publishers, 1984).

Chapter 5

1. Verse 1 of Joshua 5 is a natural conclusion to the previous story, of the Jordan crossing, begun at 3:1.

2. A highly recommended one–volume commentary is Charles F. Pfeiffer and Everett F. Harrison, eds., *The Wycliffe Bible Commentary* (Chicago: Moody Press, 1962). Another excellent commentary is D. Guthrie and J. A. Motyer, eds., *The New Bible Commentary Revised* (Grand Rapids, Michigan: Eerdmans, 1970).

Chapter 6

1. The question is unsettled as to whether the original text read "our" or "your." The basic application is the same.

Chapter 7

1. From *The Thompson Chain–Reference Bible* (Indianapolis: B. B. Kirkbride Bible Co.). Used by permission.

Chapter 8

1. Smith, *Profitable Bible Study*, 43

2. The Hebrew Old Testament contains 6,413 different words, exclusive of proper names, which represent about 1,860 Hebrew roots. The Greek New Testament contains 4,867 different words. In the English Bible there are about 6,000 different words. (One

particular English Bible version has a *total word count* of 773,693.)

3. Irving L. Jensen, *How to Profit From Bible Reading* (Chicago: Moody Press, 1985), viii.

4. Robert B. Girdlestone, *Old Testament Synonyms* (Grand Rapids, Michigan: Wm. B. Eerdmans Publishing Co., 1953), 6–7.

5. Richard C. Trench, *Synonyms of the New Testament* (Grand Rapids, Michigan: Wm. B. Eerdmans Publishing Co., 1948), vii.

6. Laura H. Wilk, *The Romance of the English Bible* (New York: Doubleday, Doran and Co., 1929), 195–96. *The New King James Bible* (Thomas Nelson, 1979) features changes regarding obsolete words, changed word meanings, punctuation, grammar, quotation marks, and other updated items.

7. Robert Young, *Analytical Concordance to the Bible* (Grand Rapids, Michigan: Wm. B. Eerdmans Publishing Company).

8. For example, Bible dictionaries and encyclopedias, and special studies (e.g., Girdlestone's and Trench's books on synonyms, cited earlier).

9. One recommended book for such a study is James H. Moulton and George Milligan, *The Vocabulary of the Greek Testament* (London: Hodder and Stoughton, 1952).

10. Ibid., 513.

Chapter 9

1. *The Zondervan Topical Bible* (Grand Rapids, Michigan: Zondervan, 1969).